Disruptive Leadership
Apple and the Technology of
Caring Deeply—Nine Keys to
Organizational Excellence and
Global Impact

Disruptive Leadership
Apple and the Technology of Caring Deeply—Nine Keys to Organizational Excellence and Global Impact

Rich Kao

CRC Press
Taylor & Francis Group

CRC Press is an imprint of the
Taylor & Francis Group, an **informa** business
A PRODUCTIVITY PRESS BOOK

CRC Press
Taylor & Francis Group
6000 Broken Sound Parkway NW, Suite 300
Boca Raton, FL 33487-2742

© 2018 by Richard Kao
CRC Press is an imprint of Taylor & Francis Group, an Informa business

No claim to original U.S. Government works

Printed on acid-free paper

International Standard Book Number-13: 978-1-138-57656-8 (Hardback)
International Standard Book Number-13: 978-0-203-73117-8 (eBook)

Visit the Taylor & Francis Web site at
http://www.taylorandfrancis.com

and the CRC Press Web site at
http://www.crcpress.com

This book is dedicated to my wife and kids for their support and encouragement. They were my audience of five that cheered me on and kept me going through the entire writing process. Thanks to Memie, Kimmie, Heidi, Holly, and Matt. You are the best.

Special thanks to all those who have taken the leadership journey with me, helping to validate and crystallize the ideas given in this book. Without your insights and participation, this book would not be possible. You have taught me the preeminent value of caring deeply and its vital connection to leadership.

Credits: Heidi Kao (Boot Camp Illustrations)

Contents

Introduction: The Technology of Caring Deeply

One of the ways that I believe people express their appreciation to the rest of humanity is to make something wonderful and put it out there. [In] the act of making something with a great deal of care and love, something is transmitted... That's what's going to keep Apple, Apple.[1]

–**Steve Jobs**

We've all touched it. The Mac. The iPod. The iPhone. The iPad. The pine tables. It's beautiful. It's gorgeous. It delights. By all rights, these devices represent revolutions in personal computing, music, mobile communication, tablets, and retail. So disruptive are Apple's products to each respective industry, *Wired's* Mat Honan stated of its founder, "Steve Jobs didn't simply shake up industries; he fundamentally traumatized them."[2]

In 2004, Apple's market value was less than $10 billion. Shortly after Jobs passed away (October 5, 2011), Apple went on to become the most valuable company in the world, worth nearly $800 billion[3,4] with a path to $1 trillion valuation in sight. To put that in perspective, Apple was worth more than Microsoft, Google, Amazon, and Facebook combined.[5] Its market capitalization was worth more than the entire Russian stock market or all the companies listed in the Portugal, Ireland, Greece, and Spain exchanges added together.[4,6]

Along the way, Apple amassed a cash holding of over $250 billion, an amount never previously accumulated by any company.[7] And as measured by its love affair with the consumer, 800 million itunes users with credit card information are on file with Apple.[8,9] No company has ever reached such heights of success. It's extraordinary by every measure.

Yet despite the throngs that line up for days to buy and behold the latest incarnation of Apple's hit machine, there is another technology behind the technology that represents Apple's true power and genius. It's the **technology of caring deeply**. Behind the silicon chips, unibody frames, and exquisite touchable panes of glass, behind the award-winning marketing and crowded, buzzing stores, the technology of caring deeply is what inspires it all. While it may be tempting to view caring as a soft skill, it will be seen how it is the key to world-changing activity and how it creates a wave of powerful leadership and organizational disciplines. Caring is anything but soft. It changes the world.

Leaders live to make a difference. When they see a need, feel a hurt, or discern a problem, they take off in pursuit of change. They are history chasers, and organizations live or die by them. This is why leadership is one of the most intensely studied subjects. The world can't function without leaders. It's been said, "We get up in the morning, open the newspaper, turn on our computer, radio, or television, and discover what actions leaders all over the world have taken. It is integral to rural tribal cultures as well as modern industrialized nations. Leadership is all around us."[10]

In this vein, leadership is the new social science. Leadership is one of the most social activities on the planet. Nothing happens without leadership, good or bad. And the associated research around leadership has been vigorous and intense. Over the last 100 years, more than 200 definitions of leadership have been given. More than 65 classifications of leadership have been formulated. Business books by the hundreds are published each year on the subject. Graduate programs of all kinds—from business schools to seminaries—now offer advanced degrees in leadership. Leadership has emerged as a distinct area of academic study, worthy of our attention and the conferring of letters.

***

Leadership is the activity of getting things done through a collective people. But where does it start? At the core of this book is the idea that all disruptive activity begins in the deepest parts of a leader. The journey of leadership with its incumbent responsibilities and burden is not an easy one. To disrupt a market, invent a new product, conceive a new service, or create a new system takes a gargantuan amount of effort. While there may be distinctly capitalistic motivations, in the end, disruption is a labor of love. Money is not the motivation. Status is not the motivation. Something greater is. Freedom. Justice. Healing. Enlightenment. Transformation. No money can buy that. This is the notion behind caring deeply, which serves as the backbone to the leadership framework that is to follow. Caring deeply is the "command and control center" that touches every aspect of disruption, from ideation to realization. At some point, everything traces back to the question "How deeply do I care?" It is the gut check for every step of the journey.

Of course people care about things in different ways and in different measures. They care about their pets. They care about their sports teams. They care about their jobs. But the caring referred to here is of the highest kind. It's a caring that leads to action—being so moved about something as to actually doing something about it. It's caring enough to take responsibility for a situation: to lead and, yes, even to disrupt.

Disruption is a strong word. By definition, it means "disturbance or problems that interrupt an event, activity, or process." Typically, disturbances are associated with the negative—bad classroom behavior, unruly customers, protestors, riots. But this is not how disruption is used here. **Disruption here is taken to mean a force for good—a force for change that makes things better, either by displacing or overthrowing the old, or by creating new ways, things, thinking, or methods**. Harvard professor Clay Christensen first connoted disruption as a positive dynamic by connecting it to innovation.[11] By doing so, he created a whole new way of understanding business. Arguably, his ideas have become the seeds of the current design thinking and lean start-up movements. In this book, the concept of disruption is expanded upon by applying it to the arenas of organizational and leadership development.

***

This book is designed to speak on two levels—specific and universal. The specific level is about the exemplary outworking of disruptive leadership as seen at Apple since its founding in 1976. But it goes beyond that. Apple does not have a monopoly on these principles, nor did they invent them. Rather, they have validated universal principles that will work wherever leadership is needed. The principles of disruption work not only in business, but in educational, political, military, athletic, and nonprofit sectors. They work in Fortune 500 companies or in start-ups. They work in developing countries and developed countries. They work no matter the age, race, or gender. They work wherever there is a dream.

While Apple serves as the primary pillar in this book, other corporate examples are used to amplify key points. As of late, there are many outstanding companies to choose from—Uber, Airbnb, Xiaomi, Snapchat, Pinterest—all part of the new "unicorn" companies with billion dollar or more valuations. They all have the look and feel of being highly disruptive. However, many of these shining stars will not be cited for statistical reasons. Establishing an enduring company is not an easy task. According to the U.S. Bureau of Labor Statistics, nearly 70% of all businesses fail within ten years.[12,13] All of the aforementioned companies haven't reached their tenth birthday. They are still "kids." Indeed, Facebook and Twitter barely make the ten-year-old cutoff. This is not to dismiss or doubt the future success of these unicorns, but they are deliberately excluded here so as to give them more time to establish their credentials. Instead, other stellar examples will be drawn upon from a variety of industries: Union Square (food), IKEA (furniture), ING Direct (banking), Nike (athletics), Starbucks (coffee), Zappos (shoes), and more.

***

Finally, this book is meant to be a "quiet book," one that goes behind the roar commonly associated with Apple. Countless excellent books, articles, and blogs have been written about Apple (even movies have been produced). This is meant to be an "under the radar" book, a synthesis book that pulls together the disparate aspects of leadership that have been previously noted but in a *unified* manner so the sweep of disruptive leadership can be better understood. There is certainly more than one way to parse and construct disruptive leadership, but the idea is not so much to perfectly define it as it is to provide a picture so leaders can add their own insights and narrative to the theme. The hope is one's own leadership journey will be duly enhanced, deviously disruptive, and marvelously impactful.

Author

Rich Kao is a veteran leader of 30 years and lover of dynamic start-ups. He has held research and teaching positions at Kallestad Labs (Hoffman-La Roche), 3M, and EQUIP and is currently a managing director with Measurement Technology Laboratories in Minneapolis, Minnesota, a high-tech company specializing in measuring air quality monitoring. He is founding pastor of Five Stones Church in Vancouver, British Columbia, a member of the Cabinet of Canadians, and is currently serving the Trudeau Administration on issues of religious freedom and human rights. He has started several humanitarian organizations using aid and leadership platforms to serve the underprivileged in Asia. He is also CEO of a new green company, Paper Hive City, which is a design studio specialized in converting paperboard into consumer and business products. He has a BA in biology from Carleton College, an MS in immunology from the University of Minnesota, and a doctorate in leadership (D.SL) from Regent University.

1

Disruption Takes Leadership

It's alright to be Goliath, but always act like David.[1]

—Phil Knight, Nike founder

Disruption does not happen by itself. It takes leadership. Disruption is a necessary response to the inertia that is all around us. Goliath, from the biblical story of David and Goliath, is a powerful symbol of that inertia, weight, and deceleration. Goliath represents the old order. David represents the new order. Goliath is big and ugly and must be vanquished. David is new and fresh and has never been seen before. David is unanticipated and unconventional. Goliath is foreboding and standing in the way. Goliath is attitudinal, systemic, and entrenched; he stands in the way of progress and change. David comes to replace Goliath. David comes to disrupt.

It's been said that Apple founder Steve Jobs' "natural inclination was to position himself as the critic, the rebel, the visionary, the lithe and nimble David against the stodgy Goliath of whatever powers might be."[2] This David and Goliath metaphor, however, is more than an apt descriptor. It is actually a leadership school, pregnant with insights on how disruption, organizational excellence, and caring deeply are connected. Steve Jobs understood this intuitively, but David, the shepherd boy, was an exciting first mover on this subject. And as we shall see, his epic story intersects with Apple at various telling points along the way.

THE CHAMPION FROM BETHLEHEM

Who is this uncircumcised Philistine that he should defy the armies of the living God?[3]

—David in speaking of Goliath

Thus began the tipping point for one of the most famous battles in history.[4] For forty days and forty nights, once in the morning and once in the evening the renowned Philistine giant taunted the armies of Israel. Locked in a pitched battle for supremacy in the region, Goliath set the terms according to ancient battle rules. He, the Philistine champion, would take on the opposing side's champion, and the side that lost would become servants to the winning side. These terms of engagement were referred to as the "contest of champions."[5]

Day after day, Goliath's nearly ten-foot frame loomed large. King Saul and his men stood petrified in the presence of the menacing figure. No one dared take on the Philistine champion. His coat of armor, made of bronze, weighed 125 pounds, while his spear, the size of a beam, was topped off with a 15-pound iron tip. So strong and imposing was Goliath that his very sight induced paralysis. Then by chance, a young boy, David, while shuttling food from Bethlehem to his brothers on the front lines, happened upon Goliath issuing his morning challenge. Even though the armies of Israel were moving in battle formation and "shouting the war cry," whenever Goliath appeared, Saul's soldiers fled in fear. David was incredulous. Why were the men scattering? What was there to fear? This uncircumcised Philistine was defying the armies of the living God. What would be done for "the man who kills this Philistine, and takes away the reproach from Israel?"[6] Saul's men were stunned. Did this young lad intend to take on the giant?

Word trickled back to King Saul. A shepherd boy was indicating his willingness to fight Goliath, so an interview was hastily arranged. David repeated his words before the king. There was nothing to fear. He would take on the Philistine giant. The king listened and was impressed by his courage but dissuaded by his unimpressive appearance and lack of military training. But David would not be deterred. He argued that his field experience among the flocks was more than adequate. He had successfully, while protecting his father's sheep, killed both a lion and a bear. Goliath would be just like one of them. The same God that "delivered me from the paw of the lion and from the paw of the bear, He will deliver me from the hand of this Philistine."[7] David pressed home his point and Saul was won over. Quickly, the king had him suited up to confront Goliath.

But the weapons and armor issued were too big. There were no sizes small enough for young David, and he struggled to maneuver in them. Confidently David told the king he had to set them aside. He would use his own innovative military gear, a highly honed, leather-bound sling—tested and developed in his own secret "pastoral laboratory." He had five smooth stones in his shepherd's pouch. He had all the artillery and ammunition he needed for victory. The king, bemused and unsure of this new combat tool, nevertheless consented.

With shepherd rod and sling in hand, David proceeded quickly into battle against Goliath, and as the text describes, felled the famed strongman with a single shot to the forehead. So lethal was the high-velocity stone that it rendered Goliath instantly unconscious. With the giant on the ground, David finished the job with military efficiency, cutting off Goliath's head with the giant's own sword. The Philistine champion was vanquished. The champion from Bethlehem had won. David had overcome all odds and secured the most improbable of victories. History was made and a hero was born.

But is this how the story goes? Certainly, this is one of the primary narratives and one of the most inspirational ones. However, when viewed from a wider frame, there is a larger story at work. It's not just an "overcoming-all-odds" story; it's a story about leadership. When David stepped into the fray, he was stepping into a leadership vacuum. Israel had crossed a crucial point in their history. Instead of being ruled by judges, they were now led by their first king. The people had cried out for a king so they could be like the nations that were around them.[8] Saul had the privilege to be Israel's first monarch, and he was appointed to this highest office so "our king may judge us and go out before us and fight our battles."[9] Saul was to be Israel's supreme general, their inspiration, and the one that would lead them to victory. Early in his reign, Saul did just that, accruing victories over the Ammonites and Amalekites.[10] But as the crucial battle with the Philistines unfolded, Saul could not muster the necessary leadership. Now Israel's national security was on the line.[11] The Philistines sensed the wavering and weakness in the new king and sought to exploit it. Goliath was sent in as the chief intimidator.

In this context, the battle between David and Goliath represented something more than a legendary battlefield victory. At a higher level, this confrontation was about an emerging new order being intimidated by the old order. Israel was seeking to establish itself afresh under a new monarchial system, but the Philistine rule was seeking to snuff it out. Enter David. Israel was stuck and it required a breakthrough. Anytime an organization wants to break into new territory, it has to have a disruptive leader. This is exactly what we see in Steve Jobs during his time at Apple. He was a tech version of David. The pirate of Silicon Valley shared a deep connection with the "ruddy young boy" from Bethlehem.[12] But the story does not end there. Just as David was aiming for something higher than unveiling products never seen before, so was Steve Jobs.

―――――

LONG LIVE THE ORGANIZATION

> My goal has always been not only to make great products, but to build great companies.[13]

―Steve Jobs

This quote is telling for the word "always," as it reveals what was Jobs' lifelong obsession. Jobs' intent was to not just make great products but to build great companies. His aim was not to just create disruptive products but to create disruptive organizations. This finer but key point is commonly missed in the excitement over the insanely innovative widgets typically associated with Jobs. **This is why this book looks at the organizational side of Jobs.** The goal is to identify a comprehensive road map for creating insanely great companies. Jobs was more than a builder of breakthrough products, he was above all the builder of great organizations. His passion was not just Apple products but Apple the company. Here again, the David and Goliath analogy explains how Jobs' organizational powers came to be.

DAVID: A MAN OF THE HEART

God sees not as man sees, for man looks at the outward appearance, but the Lord looks at the heart.

—I Sam. 16:7

David was a man of the heart. He was a man who cared deeply and felt strongly. His whole impetus for engaging Goliath came from his love for God.[14] Who would dare defame the name of God? From a young age, while tending the flock in the rolling hills of Bethlehem, David developed a friendship and kinship with God that was strong and loyal. Being frequently alone, he capitalized on that solitude to think, ponder, and nurture his faith. The closer he grew to God, the more fond he became of Jehovah, Israel's beautiful, awe-inspiring God. And the more he cared, the more he understood where his passion lay. Without realizing it, a foundation for leadership was being built in his life. It would be a foundation so strong that it would catapult him above his peers, even above the elite soldiers of the day. Caring deeply would be his distinguishing mark. It would take him from the Valley of Elah, where his fame first arose from defeating Goliath, to the royal throne in Jerusalem. David's innovative slingshot might have been his calling card, but his real legacy would become his reign as king. David's passion for God led him from his father's humble pasture to the boardroom of Israel, Inc. David's tenure was the most beloved period in Israel's history. He became the gold standard by which all kings would be measured. David's storied life began as a teenage projectile warrior,[15] but it ended with building the greatest dynasty ever. David succeeded greatly because he cared deeply.

The analogy is clear. Like David, Jobs' deep sense of care led him to create the most successful company in history. Apple wasn't about vainglory. It was about making a mark and making one's life count. Famous for saying he wanted to "make a dent in the universe," Jobs remarkably did just that, as Apple would become the most valuable, most profitable, and most respected company in the world. And in so doing, a new clarity would emerge as to how disruption works.

A NEW FOCAL POINT

Leadership is easy. All you have to do is find something worth dying for.[16]

—Hugh Macleod, business cartoonist and best-selling author

At its core, the idea of caring deeply is about being so gripped and captivated by something that one is willing to give his or her life to it. In every person, there is a "caring deeply gene," i.e., something that so moves a person that it becomes the delight and passion of their life. "This is what I was created for" becomes the exclamation. It's that gene that allows us to find meaning in life. This caring gene is, of course, different for every person. This is why disruption occurs in so many places in so many different ways. For some, the caring gene revolves around justice. For others it's about mercy. Others may revel in saving the environment or eradicating a disease. Yet others want to make people laugh or create the best culinary experience. The nodes of caring are as vast as the human experience, and the world needs everyone to find their node. This caring gene is what can make every person a leader of significance.

In the 1900s, the literature on leadership focused on command and control models. Today the dialogue revolves around shared goals, soft power, and influence. Each iteration of leadership has a certain focal point—from skills to traits to styles—that provides an organizing thread. The idea of caring deeply is that, while implied in other leadership paradigms (e.g., in great man, charismatic, and transformational theories), yet when it is called out as its own focal point, it creates a new paradigm with many personal and organizational implications. When these implications are placed in a unifying model, it then has power to instruct and guide leaders to perform at their highest levels. Here, this unifying model is called the Disruptive Leadership Model (DLM) (Figure 1.1), and it represents how caring serves as the wellspring to disruption and as the critical driver of alignment for organizational effectiveness.

According to this model, caring deeply is not just an emotion; it is a technology that works at the deepest level. Formally defined, technology is "a *manner* of accomplishing a task using processes, methods or knowledge."[17] Caring is thus the "*inspired* manner" by which things get done.

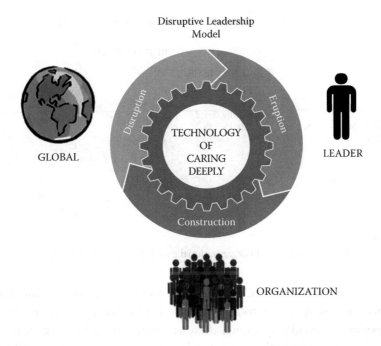

FIGURE 1.1
Disruptive Leadership Model.

Genetically speaking, DNA is the code that gives expression to species. It determines how a species looks, lives, and functions. DNA may be invisible to the eye, but it is the magical chromosomal recipe for what is made manifest. Caring deeply is the DNA of the leadership species, the "double helix" of disruptive leaders. Caring technology is not squishy or random; rather, it provides direction, structure, and know-how that lead to powerful and creative outcomes.

There are three phases to the DLM. The first phase is individual. It's inner. It's personal. It's developing and accruing the mental pictures and emotional fuel that precipitates leadership action. This is the ERUPTION phase. The second phase is organizational. This is about gathering a team and building a company that will embark on change. It's about creating the mission and vision to overcome the Goliaths. This is the CONSTRUCTION phase. The third phase is impact, making a difference. This is where the old is vanquished and the new is established. This is where momentum and sea change take place—within industries, companies, departments, or even inside PTA committees. This is the DISRUPTION phase.

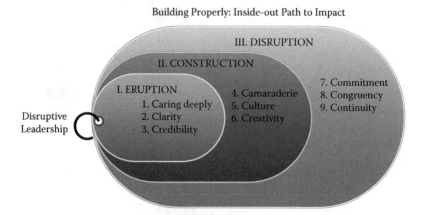

Building Properly: Inside-out Path to Impact

FIGURE 1.2
Key chain diagram: Nine keys to organizational excellence and global impact.

This simple triphasic model is played out over and over again through disruptive organizations. In total, nine aspects of this caring technology will be explored. Broadly speaking, these attributes move from an inside-to-outside progression: (1) caring deeply, (2) clarity, and (3) credibility are part of the ERUPTION phase; (4) core team, (5) culture, and (6) creativity occur in the CONSTRUCTION phase; and (7) commitment, (8) congruency, and (9) continuity take place in the DISRUPTION phase. These nine elements, however, are fluid, moving between phases at times, since each attribute can act upon or reinforce one another. Another way to visualize the model is given in Figure 1.2.

The thesis of the DLM is that there can be no remarkable display of leadership, no stellar organization, and no global impact without deep abiding care. That is where the power is.

Section I

Eruption: Individual Arena

Progression to Impact

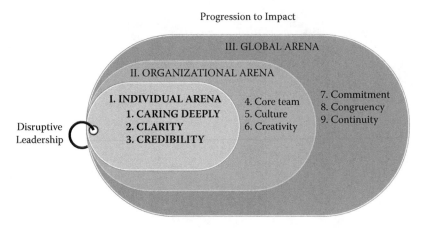

FIGURE S.I
Key chain.

2

Caring Deeply:
The Plumb Line of Excellence

The most important thing is that you care.[1]

—Jony Ive, Chief Design Officer, Apple

Where does caring deeply come from? How does it come about in a leader? Intuitively, we know that caring is not made in a lab or bought in a store. It's not something that can be manufactured or synthesized. Rather, it is something that comes about more randomly and freely, yet profoundly. It begins with how one interacts with life.

LOVE FOR BEAUTY

As Walter Isaacson, Jobs' official biographer, noted, Jobs was a man deeply curious and absorbed in his world. Whether it was gardening, building fences, tinkering with electronics, or observing the tract homes he grew up in, Jobs was keenly observant and self-aware, clear about his likes and dislikes. He loved walking to school and earning money from his newspaper route, traditional rites of passage, but he also gave expression to his wild side by taking drugs and seeking for enlightenment in India.[2] Although he never finished college, one of the courses that made a great impact on Jobs was a calligraphy class that introduced him to the art of lettering and font-making.[3] Jobs would later state his appreciation for great calligraphy was built "into [all] the Mac[s]. It was the first computer with beautiful typography."[4] Jobs also came of age through the antiwar years in the 1970s where the music of Bob Dylan and The Beatles left an indelible mark on him.[5]

Jobs' zest for life made him strongly opinionated about what was beautiful or ugly, convictions that would later fuel his management style at Apple.

Jobs credited much of Apple's genius to this kind of experiential living, saying, "The reason we were able to come up with great ideas is that we had more experiences or had thought more about our experiences than other people. The broader one's understanding of the human experience, the better designs we will have."[6] While Apple was known as a technology company, at its core, it was motivated by Jobs' beauty aesthetic.

In books such as *Tinkertoys* by Michael Michalko, brainstorming and creative thinking techniques are presented as "in the moment" kind of skills to be used.[7] But these cannot compare with deeper convictions embedded in one's thoughts and emotions regarding beauty—as possessed by Jobs—since these become innate governors. Hence, making sure the color of a package was perfect or obsessing if sapphire or Gorilla Glass™ should be paired with a phone's touch transitive surface[8] was eminently important and worth the time.

Jobs appreciated beauty wherever it could be found. Whether it was the supple leather wrapped around the steering wheel of a Mercedes or the perfect symmetry of a watch dial, his delight in beautiful things provided the ongoing motivation to improve the world and make it better in ways not seen before. Beauty was the highest-octane fuel Jobs could find, and it was the only fuel he would put in his tank.

PASSION FOR SIMPLICITY

From the stream, he chose five smooth stones.[9]

—David's implements of victory

David killed Goliath with utter simplicity. No fancy bows and arrows, no fancy gear. Just simple stones, fashioned and polished by a river until they became perfectly smooth, perfect to hold, and perfect for bringing down giants. David's "simple technology" was light-years ahead of the competition. Simple is what made David so good.

What does "good" look like? Is it delivering flowers at noon, when no one is home or at 6 pm when the recipient can personally receive a gift of thoughtfulness? Is it warehousing inventory in one giant supercenter or in smaller regional centers? Is it organizing a library of digital songs on a microdisk, or doing it in the cloud?[10] For Steve Jobs, "good" was a headphone jack yielding a satisfying click when plugging in the earphones on the iPod.[11] For Jobs, good meant spending 6 months to refine the scrollbars in the operating system.[12] For Jobs, good prevailed when simplicity emerged.

Apple lived and died by this principle. For any challenges placed in front of them, it was about reducing it to its simplest, cleanest form. Any recommendation that did not make something more intuitive or easy was vetoed. Jonathan Ive, chief designer at Apple, stated, "To a lot of people [our] products seem obvious. They are so plain and simple, there seems to be no design involved at all. There are no frills or accouterments that trumpet the design process. That's the point. The task is to solve incredibly complex problems and make their resolution appear inevitable and incredibly simple, so you have no sense how difficult the thing was."[13]

As Jobs said, the work of simplicity is not an easy task. "Simple can be harder than complex. You have to work hard to get your thinking clean to make it simple. But it's worth it in the end because once you get there, you can move mountains."[14] For Jobs, the purpose of problem solving was to make something simpler, more elegant, and more natural. Simplicity was the ultimate sophistication.[15] As Segall writes, "Simplicity was religion at Apple. It wasn't just a design principle, it was a value that permeated every level of the organization."[16] Jobs was the simplicity enforcer, using "the simple stick" to bat away anything that had the smell of cluster, stupidity, or ugliness. Hence, the iPhone would have only one home button, not three, even though the iPhone was a marriage of three devices—a phone, a music player, and a web surfer.[17] When Jobs saw the first prototype of the iPod, he was unconvinced that it was small or compact enough. He thought the engineers could do better, to which they thought otherwise. In a dramatic moment of confrontation, he proceeded to drop the prototype in a nearby fish tank. As the device sank, bubbles floated to the top. Said Jobs, "Those are air bubbles. That means there's space in there. Make it smaller."[18] Game over.

Where does this kind of leadership come from? What does a leader see when he considers a problem to be solved, a widget to be made, or an industry to be changed? Inner vision is the key. For Jobs, simplicity and beauty were the unmovable and sacred pillars of excellence.

POWER OF NURTURE: ON BEING AN ARTIST AND CRAFTSMAN

He loved doing things right. He even cared about the look of the parts you couldn't see.[2]

—Steve Jobs on his dad's sense of craftsmanship.

Jobs did not see himself as a purveyor of technology. He saw himself as an artist. His passion was for Apple to "stand at the intersection of technology and liberal arts."[19] At an early age it was his adoptive father, Paul Jobs, that instilled in Jobs a deep sense of care for even the smallest details. Whether it was mending fences or fixing cars, the elder Jobs taught his son to care about all the parts that made the whole, not just the things that could be seen. Jobs' father taught him how important it was "to craft the backs of cabinets and fences properly even though they were hidden."[2] Later, Jobs would insist that the internal circuit boards on the Mac be lined perfectly though no one would ever notice[20]; that all robots at the NeXT plant be painted in coordinated shades of gray and black, which required four applications of paint to make it look right[21]; and that the iPhone be completely redesigned just as it was about to be launched because the casing competed with the display "instead of getting out of the way."[22] Most other companies would have shipped, but for Jobs the product wasn't perfect. As Jobs confessed to Ive, "I didn't sleep last night because I realized I just don't love it." Jobs couldn't go to market with a product he didn't love. As Jobs would say, "Artists sign their work"[23] and the iPhone didn't have all of Jobs' soul in it.

As Jobs plied his craft in ways unseen before, little did he know that on the other side of the pond, there was an Englishman who had the same mindset for meticulous care and excellence. He too was greatly influenced by his father, and he too would yearn for a place where his highest design ideals could be realized. As events would unfold, one champion of care would soon meet another.

ELEVATING "SOCIAL" TO NEW HEIGHTS

Jony was interested in getting things right and fit for purpose. He was completely interested in humanizing technology.[24]

—Peter Phillips, designer at Roberts Weaver Group, London's leading design firm.

In his pursuit of changing the world, there was no one closer to Jobs than Jony Ive. Jobs' passion to bring liberal arts and technology together in breathtaking ways had a perfect companion in Ive. When Ive first encountered the Mac as a rising design star and university student, he was deeply impacted.

From the first, Jony was astounded at how much easier to use the Mac was than anything else he had tried. The care the machine's designers took to shape the whole user experience struck him; he felt an immediate connection to the machine and, more important, to the soul of the enterprise. It was the first time he felt the humanity of a product. 'It was such a dramatic moment and I remember it so clearly,' he said. 'There was a real sense of the people who made it.[25]

Ive would further elaborate:

I started to learn more about Apple, how it had been founded, its values and its structure. The more I learned about this cheeky almost rebellious company, the more it appealed to me, as it unapologetically pointed to an alternative in the complacent and creatively bankrupt industry. Apple stood for something and had a reason for being that wasn't just about making money.[26]

Though it would take a few years before Ive finally ended up at Apple, his connection with Jobs was strong and immediate. When Jobs returned to Apple after his firing 12 years earlier, his first impulse was to get rid of the company's designers... until he walked into Ive's design studio. The studio embodied everything Jobs was looking for—a beehive of activity that was packed with prototypes, forms, and shapes that mirrored the elegant aspirations of the soft-spoken designer. Ive would soon become Jobs' partner in crime. Jobs began to stop by daily to see what was happening in the studio, and having lunch together became their regular routine.[27] Their bond was so strong and unique, Laurene Powell, Jobs' wife, said, "Jony had special status. He would come by our house, and our families became close. Most people in Steve's life are replaceable. But not Jony."[27] As Jobs described it:

> The difference that Jony has made, not only at Apple but in the world, is huge. He is a wickedly intelligent person in all ways. He understands business concepts, marketing concepts. He picks stuff up just like that, click. He understands what we do at our core better than anyone. If I had a spiritual partner at Apple, it's Jony. Jony and I think up most of the products together and then pull others in and say, "Hey what do you think about this?" He gets the big picture as well as the most infinitesimal details about each product. And he understands that Apple is a product company. He's not just a designer. That's why he works directly for me. He has more operational power than anyone else at Apple except me. There's no one who can tell him what to do or to butt out. That's the way I set it up.[27]

Ive shared Jobs' passion to make technology accessible to the masses and to cultivate designs that made products infinitely more human and social. With Jobs, he elevated the connection between man and machine to new heights. It wasn't about putting a nice "skin" on a set of engineer specs. Design was meant to be a distinctly human activity, or as design thinking gurus like Tim Brown would later call it, "putting people first."[28]

The idea of "starting with people" was serious business for Ive.[29] For him, it meant putting in the utmost care into any design. "I always understood the beauty of things made by hand. I came to realize that what was really important was the care that was put into it. What I really despise is when I sense some carelessness in a product."[30]

For Ive, the conception of a product began with a story, a metaphor, to capture the emotion to be conveyed. This meant becoming deeply empathetic with the user and discerning what connected them to the product. While still a design student, Ive showed an uncanny ability to zero in on what engaged users at a deeper level than practical functionality. Tasked with creating a new line of pens, he noticed how people loved to fiddle with their pens. Instead of trying to eliminate this proclivity for fiddling, he catered to it by creating a clicking mechanism at the top of the pen so people could enjoy their hand-held diversions. This created a "fun factor" and an emotional connection to the pens.[31] For Ive, there was a sense that "tactile elements" were crucial to creating a bond, an approach that would later show itself strongly in Apple's products.[31] Fiddling was part of the story. It was empathy at work. This was Ive's caring technology in full bloom.

Not to be forgotten, this caring showed itself not only in big ways but also in small ways. Ive's attention to detail even drilled down to the seemingly mundane task of unpacking a product. Previously unidentified, Ive and Jobs zeroed in on how opening a product could be an essential part of the user experience. As Ive put it, "Packaging can be theater, it can create a story."[32] No designer had ever connected packaging to the idea of theater. This was powerful insight at work, driven by a desire to delight the user. As millions of YouTube videos attest to the moment of unboxing is indeed a wonderful and now expected part of enjoying a product. As biographer Kahney writes, "Caring enough to commit the enormous time and effort to get something right has always been Jony's hallmark."[33] Excellence never had a better partner.

 BOOT CAMP #1: PURSUING EXCELLENCE

1. What drives you to excellence? Is care at the center of that motivation? Why or why not?

2. Do you have an excellent organization? Rate the quality of your company on a scale of 1 (poor) to 10 (excellent) _____. If your company is not a 10, how can caring deeply lift your organization to another level?

3. What inspired you most from Jobs' and Ive's commitment to caring deeply? How can you apply this to yourself and your organization?

3

Clarity: Caring Deeply Has a Goal

The Macintosh is inside of me, and I've got to get it out and turn it into a product.[1]

—Steve Jobs

HIGH-DEFINITION CLARITY

To move mountains or shake up the status quo, a leader needs clear vision. He must know the target he is moving toward with great clarity. As experts have written, vision is crucial to paradigmatic shifts and changes. Leaders have a vision of a preferred future. Burt Nanus, a frequent collaborator with Warren Bennis, described four characteristics of an effective vision: (1) it attracts commitment and energizes people, (2) creates meaning for followers, (3) establishes a standard of excellence, and (4) helps transport people to the future.[2] In *The Leadership Challenge,* Kouzes and Posner write, "Leaders hold in their mind ideas and visions of what can be. They have a sense of what is uniquely possible."[3] When asked, "What could be worse than being born blind?" Helen Keller replied, "To have sight without vision."[4]

Possessing a compelling vision is an indisputable quality for leaders, and communicating that vision to followers "may well be the most important act of the transformational leader."[2] When Jobs distilled his vision into one sentence, "The Macintosh is inside of me, and I've got to get it out,"[1] it was his vision in high definition. Caring was not just a feeling or aspiration, it had a concrete goal. Jobs liked to say, he was a "product guy."[5]

That was his nonnegotiable. He would create things that people could touch, feel, and connect to.

LAYING HOLD OF THE HIGHER VALUE

We do it not to make money.

—**Steve Jobs**

Probing deeper, there is an even more powerful foundation to clarity. Jobs would frequently say Apple's goal was not to make money.[6] For the CEO of a publically traded company, to say this openly and frequently was a bold move, but it represented Jobs' true feelings. Money was a by-product of success but not the goal of the company. This is the principle of living by a higher value. Jobs believed in the axiom that if you took care of the top line, the bottom line would take care of itself. Ironically, this principle teaches to *not* aim for success or riches. Rather, it teaches what is primary is to secure the value proposition. Money, of course, is essential to running any organization or business. But the real value is found elsewhere. Securing the value proposition is about finding the human component that genuinely excites people. For Apple, that was making delightful products. Legions of fans pulling all-nighters to play with their latest Apple product bear witness to the bond Apple products have created with their customers. Disruption, interestingly and paradoxically, comes by not aiming for it.

Jobs' leadership embodied a relentless pursuit of the higher value, and he would regularly get his point across with the saltiness of a sailor. His disdain for ugly, thoughtless products would drip like venom from a snake. When it came to innovating the iPod, Jobs stated

> The older I get, the more I see how much motivations matter. The Zune was crappy because the people at Microsoft don't really love music or art the way we do. We won because we personally love music. We made the iPod for ourselves, and when you're doing something for yourself, or your best friends or family, you're not going to cheese out.[7]

In response to Google's criticism of Apple's closed-system approach, Jobs railed,

> "Well, look at the results—Android's a mess. It has different screen sizes and versions, over a hundred permutations." Even if Google's approach might eventually win in the marketplace, Jobs found it repellent. "I like being responsible for the whole user experience. *We do it not to make money. We do it because we want to make great products*, not crap like Android."[8]

To work at Apple meant that you bought into the message and the mission. There was no confusion as to why one would want to join Apple. Jobs' idealism and artistic vision were so clear at Apple that people were willing to sweat blood for the company. The welcome letter to new employees made sure of this:

> There's work and there's your life work. The kind of work that has your fingerprints all over it. The kind of work that you'd never compromise on. That you'd sacrifice a weekend for. You can do that kind of work at Apple. People don't come here to play it safe. They come here to swim in the deep end. They want their work to add up to something. Something big. Something that couldn't happen anywhere else. Welcome to Apple.[9]

LOSING 20/20 VISION

He flipped [the] priorities.[10]

—Jobs in describing CEO Sculley, after Jobs' ouster at Apple.

That Apple's success was directly related to Jobs' sense of care is seen in when considering the tenures of John Sculley, Michael Spindler, and Gil Amelio, the three CEOs of Apple during Steve Jobs' absence from 1985 to 1996.[2] In those 11 years, Apple accumulated $1.86 billion in losses and was 90 days away from bankruptcy.[11] This was the same Apple company that brought the personal computer to the masses in years previous. No matter how much these successors tried to continue the company's magical ways, it was not to be had. The creative culture of Apple drained away as quickly as its profits. Why? Because they did not possess the 20/20 vision that Jobs had for its deepest values. The heart and soul of Apple products left when Jobs did. These CEOs were technocrats and bottom-line think-ers, not driven by caring deeply.[12] Jobs said of Sculley, "[He] flipped these priorities to where the goal was to make money. It's a subtle difference, but it ends up meaning *everything*: the people you hire, who gets promoted, what you discuss in meetings."[10] The DNA that Jobs had instilled in the company had disappeared.

But as history would have it, Jobs was able to return to Apple and right the ship in ways no one could have imagined. Apple had already been wildly successful under Jobs' first tenure, but now it was going to be turbocharged. Not only did Jobs get it right the first time, he was now coming back with a vengeance. And while Jobs was proving the power of clarity in the tech world, the same principles would find themselves percolating in a decidedly different arena. A young Jewish upstart from St. Louis, Danny Meyer, was about to make his mark for the love of food.

A NEW FORCE IN RESTAURANTS: UNION SQUARE CAFE

Restaurants are a notoriously tough and competitive business. More res-taurants fail than succeed—80% in the first five years[13]—and even fewer become famous, let alone game-changers. Danny Meyer, founder of Union Square Cafe in New York City, is an exception. Meyer and his family of res-taurants have been able to succeed at the highest levels, earning 28 James Beard Awards, three Michelin Stars and was ranked by Zagat as the most popular restaurant for 16 years. In 2016, Meyer himself was crowned the number one restaurant executive in the United States.[14] For his success, Meyer was chosen to create a new dining experience for the Museum of Modern Art in New York City. How did a young man with no restaurant background reach the top of his profession? By harnessing the power of caring and navigating the restaurant space with uncommon clarity and insight.

WOW INSIGHT

Like Jobs, Meyer would learn that building the best in the business was not about money, fame, or accolades. Rather he was motivated by something more special and deeply insightful:

> All these years later, the delights of the table continue to stimulate me as I pursue my career. But what really challenges me to get up and go to work every day...is my deep conviction about the intense human drive to provide and receive hospitality—*well beyond the world of restaurants.* Within moments of being born, most babies find themselves receiving the first four gifts of life: eye contact, a smile, a hug, and some food. We receive many other gifts in a lifetime, but few can ever surpass those first four. That first time may be the purest "hospitality transaction" we'll ever have, and it's not much of a surprise that we'll crave those gifts for the rest of our lives. I know I do.[15]

Based on this "wow insight," Meyer would go on to state what was at the core of his businesses:

> You may think, as I once did, that I'm primarily in the business of serving good food. Actually, though, *food is secondary* to something that matters even more. In the end, what's most meaningful is creating positive, uplifting outcomes for human experiences and human relationships. Business, like life, is about how you make people feel. It's that simple, and it's that hard.[16]

There it was, high-definition clarity popping up in a completely different industry, powered by a value proposition rooted in care and the human experience. Meyer was catapulted to living by a higher ideal. Building a great restaurant was not about just serving good food, as necessary and essential as that was (and which was the conventional wisdom); instead, Meyer's insight led to a powerful new paradigm. Building a world-class restaurant was actually about making people feel welcomed through the ministry of hospitality. This platform would thus become the immovable rock of Meyer's endeavors:

> Hospitality is the foundation of my business philosophy. Virtually nothing else is as important as how one is made to feel in any business transaction.

Hospitality exists when you believe the other person is on your side. The converse is just as true. Hospitality is present when something happens for you. It is absent when something happens to you. Those two simple prepositions—for and to—express it all.[17]

Meyer's penetrating insight was now connected to a goal. Serving the best food had to be connected to the spirit of hospitality. Anything less would make the food taste good, but not superb. And only superb would do.

ENDURING SUCCESS

Like Apple, Meyer would leverage his clarity into enduring success. While Union Square Cafe was Meyer's first hit in the mid-1980s, he would go on to establish Gramercy Tavern (luxury dining), Eleven Madison Park (creative fine dining), Tabla (Indian-inspired fare), Blue Smoke (barbecue), Jazz Standard (music club), and Shake Shack (burgers and frozen custard)—all hits in their own right and all validating the universality of his hospitality principles. His passion for food, first cultivated as he traveled Europe in his 20s, coalesced around his pivotal insight about hospitality, which then became the centerpiece of his organization. His fame as a restaurateur would become history. As Meyer would explain, the excellence of Union Square Hospitality Group came down to knowing what was in your core. That's where the rumblings and eruptions take place that lead to exciting ventures:

Wherever your center lies, know it, name it, stick to it, and believe in it. Everyone who works with you will know what matters to you and will respect and appreciate your unwavering values. Your inner beliefs about business will guide you through the tough times. It's good to be open to fresh approaches to solving problems. But, when you cede your core values to someone else, it's time to quit.[18]

Conversely, when you know what you're about, you never quit, because there's too much joy to be had.

BOOT CAMP #2: GOAL-SETTING

Once you know your mission of care, it's time to put meat on the bones. It's time to get tangible. What will your mission look like? For Jobs, it was to marry technology with the arts. For Meyer, it was to show hospitality by creating unforgettable dining experiences.

1. In view of what you care deeply about, write down how you want to translate your burden into something that's real and concrete.

2. Can you express your goal in a clear and concise manner? If so, what is it? If not, you need to keep honing how you will communicate it.

3. Write down the short-, mid-, and long-range milestones you need to hit to make your mission a reality.

4

Credibility: Why Should Others Follow Me in Caring?

David [was set] over the men of war, and it was pleasing in the sight of all the people.

—I Sam. 18:5

We return to the young shepherd of Israel. David's giant-slaying moment vaulted him to a leadership position he could have never anticipated. While he was doing what was natural for him (eliminating threat), the people saw something different. In David was a man they could follow. In David was a man so able that he excelled beyond even the best trained of the day. While the other captains and generals were flummoxed by how to handle Goliath, David went in and took him out with lightning speed. The people fell in love with David, and when he was placed in charge over the men of war, the people were thrilled. Who better to lead them than their new champion?

But behind the hero reception that welcomed David home, there was a special ingredient that led to his new notoriety. In hiddenness, David mastered the slinging skills that would cause him to stand out. David's win was not a fluke incident. It wasn't a one-and-done moment. He was "best in class." David's national following was rooted in personal hard work. He was proven, and he had credibility.

BE AN OUTLIER

In his book *Outlier*, Gladwell forwards the idea that world-class ability (e.g., in music, athletics, science) is not only about personal giftedness—which most people like to focus on—but that it must also be related to such important factors as a supportive environment (family, culture, opportunity) and, most tellingly, whether an individual commits himself or herself to the unsexy but utterly essential ritual of practicing, practicing, and more practicing—to the tune of 10,000 hours.[1] When 10,000 hours of practice is reached, as found by Swedish psychologist and professor Anders Ericsson, a mastery is achieved which few experience. At that point, such individuals become an "outlier" in that they break into territories of talent not previously thought possible. They are statistically outside the box. Examples of such outliers are *The Beatles* and *Microsoft* founder Bill Gates, both of whom achieved otherworldly acclaim in their respective fields because of their history of 10,000 hours of practice as musicians and in software coding.

This is a fascinating thesis and ties back to young David. He was placed in a unique environment—a solo shepherd boy with little distractions—that allowed him and forced him to perfect a skill to protect the sheep. When he presented himself to King Saul as one that could defeat Goliath, he was not just an impetuous teen with an outsized sense of bravado. He actually had cultivated a secret history of excellence. He had put in his 10,000 hours of practice.

While the sheep slept, he honed his skill as a marksman—stone after stone, night after night. He started with the thick trees and then graduated to the thinner trees. Then he began hitting the branches. After that, he could strike the buds on the branches. He would test different kinds of stones, small ones, big ones, craggy ones, polished ones. He would test their weight, how they fit into the sling. Would the acceleration of his windup be affected? Would it impact his release? How would the flight of the stone be affected? How long would the flight stay true? Then he would work on distance control. Could he be accurate from 10 yards out, 20 yards, 50 yards? Over and over, again and again, he practiced and schooled himself.

Then one day it happened. A hungry bear loomed nearby, and instinctively the flock felt the danger and began to turn restless. Their panicky movements caught David's attention, and scanning the edges of the herd, he saw the bear. Without even thinking, David reached into his pouch, loaded his sling, and in seconds the stone was whirling toward the bear. Dead aim. The stone struck the bear in the forehead, and it was killed on the spot. Safety returned to the sheep. In that moment, David was stunned by what he had done, but he also had a moment of realization. The sling in his hand wasn't just a toy, it was a weapon.

He was excited to tell his father how he saved the flock from the bear. But this didn't happen just once; there was also another scare. This time it was a lion. The lion represented a completely different challenge. It was a moving target. While the bear was stationary, David had to kill the lion while it was on the run, while it was rushing to attack the sheep. This would be a new test of his skill. Loading his sling once again, he aimed the stone several yards in front of the moving lion, and as the lion was lunging toward the flock, the raging animal ran right into the stone's path. Like the bear, the lion was instantly killed as the stone sunk into its skull.

When David recounted to the king these exploits, it represented something significant and statistically unique. David knew he had the training to succeed. What he didn't realize was that being "best in class" was a key attribute to creating credibility and followership. *Every leader needs to be an outlier in some way.*

BEST IN CLASS

While there is a dream inside every disruptive leader, the dream itself is not enough. Anyone can be a dreamer or think big. Instead, the disruptive leader must have an associated skill that matches the bigness of the dream. He must have a "best in class" skill (at least relative to the rest of the organization) to help make the dream happen. He doesn't have to be the best at everything, but he needs to be the best at one thing—the best salesman, best marketer, best thinker, best negotiator, best researcher, best innovator, best organizer. That one area in which he is best is key to his leadership platform. It's what gives his mission teeth. It's why others will respect, honor, and follow that leader. Without it, there is no credibility or pull.

Why should others care to follow? Having an outlier skill that contributes to the vision is a key glue for organizational cohesiveness.

Jobs in this regard is a fascinating study. As the head of a technology company, one would think his "best in class" skill would be as an engineer, software coder, or designer. But it was none of these things. Instead, his key skill was being the orchestra conductor.[2] While he had many stars in the orchestra, no one could bring them together to make music like Jobs. He could see the score before it was written and convince the musicians that their piece would sound magnificent. He was a master communicator and motivator who could point people to a reality they could not see, let alone believe they could contribute to. Yet time and time again, his vision of a future reality turned out to be exactly as he said it would be—world changing.

WHEN DISTORTED REALITY BECOMES ACTUAL REALITY

Jobs was famous for bending reality to his liking. Stated Bud Tribble, one of the original Macintosh software designers, "Steve had a reality distortion field. In his presence, reality is malleable. He could convince anyone of practically anything."[3] Steve Wozniak, one of the cofounders of Apple, described it as, "His reality distortion was when he had an illogical vision of the future, such as telling me that I could design the Breakout game in just a few days. You realized that it couldn't be true, but he somehow makes it true."[3] Another Macintosh team member, Debi Coleman, put it in even more vivid terms:

> "He reminded me of Rasputin. He laser-beamed in on you and didn't blink. It didn't matter if he was serving purple Kool-Aid. You drank it." But like Wozniak, she believed that the reality distortion field was empowering: It enabled Jobs to inspire his team to change the course of computer history with a fraction of the resources of Xerox or IBM. "It was a self-fulfilling distortion," she claimed. "You did the impossible, because you didn't realize it was impossible."[4]

Jobs thus had a way of turning what appeared to be distorted reality into actual reality. Failure always seemed to be looming close by for the audacity of what was being attempted, yet because Apple experienced success after success, against all odds in many cases, Jobs' legend only grew. As maddening as he could be, as a leader he was also magical. He could seemingly see around corners and take the company to places no organization had ever gone. Despite or perhaps because of his distortion field, with each product hit, Jobs became not just credible but revered. The orchestra conductor actually knew what he was doing. And when the impossible became reality, everyone wanted to get on the train. To follow Jobs was to put a dent in the universe.

DIFFERENT PATHS TO CREDIBILITY

As trail blazing as Jobs was, his example represents only one of many ways disruptive leaders create credibility, engagement, and loyalty. Leadership theory has given us a plethora of variables that help us understand the many factors that can lead to followership. One particular school of thought, traits theory, summarizes five key attributes that people look for in a leader: (1) Intelligence—the capacity to verbalize, reason, and think well; (2) Self-confidence—a sense of certainty about one's ability and skills; (3) Determination—the quality of persisting and persevering until the job is done; (4) Integrity—when a person exhibits honesty and trustworthiness; and (5) Sociability—a leader's ability to exude warmth and friendliness.[5]

Another school of thought focuses on the skills of a leader in three areas: (1) technical skills—which refers to a leader's knowledge and proficiency in a given area; (2) human skills—which speaks to the leader's ability to work with and get along with other people; and (3) conceptual skills—which highlights the leader's ability to work fluidly with concepts and ideas.[6] Placed in this theory, Jobs' outstanding virtue was his conceptual skills— the ability to assimilate all manner of information (technological, social, cultural, aesthetic) and put it into a compelling picture of what could be.

And in yet a different illustration of how credibility can be forged, a humble and steady Scandinavian by the name of Ingvar Kamprad laid the foundation for a furniture revolution by manifesting the power of being a living example.

DEMOCRATIZATION OF STYLISH FRUGALITY: IKEA

Ingvar Kamprad was born in Pjatteryd, a little hamlet in Sweden, about a 5-hour drive south from the capital city of Stockholm. He was raised on a farm near Agunnaryd, approximately 12 miles from his birthplace, which had a tiny population of just 220 people. It was here as a youngster that Kamprad first developed his business instincts, selling small sundry items like pens, pencils, and matchsticks. It was also during these formative years that Kamprad grew to love the salt of the earth, everyday kind of person. Interacting with them, living and growing up with them became the foundation of what he cared deeply about. His passion from the very beginnings of IKEA in 1943 was to be on the people's side (the IKEA initials were taken from his name plus the towns of Elmtaryd and Agunnaryd where he grew up), or as he formally put it later in his *Testament of a Furniture Dealer* (1976)

> We have decided once and for all to side with the many. All nations and societies in both the East and West spend a disproportionate amount of their resources on satisfying a minority of the population. In our line of business (home furnishings), for example, far too many of the fine designs and new ideas are reserved for a small circle of the affluent. That situation has influenced the formulation of our objectives...Sweden, our "domestic market," has become a world pioneer in that many of [our] new concepts have been devised right from the outset for the benefit of the many—all those people with limited resources. We are in the forefront of that development.[7]

In other words, Kamprad cared deeply about breaking down the wall of goods that could only be accessed by the wealthy so that all people could enjoy nice products. IKEA existed to "create a better everyday life for the many people by offering a wide range of well-designed, functional home furnishing products at prices so low that as many people as possible will be able to afford them."[7]

Like Steve Jobs and Danny Meyer, Kamprad possessed remarkable clarity about his company. IKEA would champion frugality and thriftiness in a stylish, Swedish-inspired way. As one of Kamprad's executives described, "[Kamprad] focuses on the human aspect. What motivates Ingvar is not profit alone but improving the quality of life of the people."[8] Once again, like at Apple and at Union Square, living by a higher value became the technology of care that powered IKEA to global success.

Toward its mission of creating a better everyday life for everyone, Kamprad pioneered many disruptive practices that upended the tradition-bound furniture industry:

1. IKEA broke away from the "Swedish practice of handing down cus-tom-made furniture through [the] generations" by helping young homeowners purchase "new, yet inexpensive furniture."[9]
2. In its early years, IKEA was so creative in working around the furniture cartel in Stockholm (that tried to put it out of business) that one retailer fumed, "IKEA resembles the monsters of old times. If we cut one of its heads, it soon grows another."[10] Kamprad succeeded wildly in setting up IKEA in the countryside of Sweden instead of in the big city where they'd have to cooperate with the established power brokers.
3. By selling furniture in locations outside the city (instead of in the usual downtown location), Kamprad was able to build generous parking spaces, which catered to the growing trend of people with cars and their shopping habits. It was during this time that IKEA pioneered the "cash-and-carry concept to furniture retailing," which revolved around

   The self-service concept facilitated by the wide distribution of informa-tive catalogs, the use of explanatory tickets on display merchandise, and the knock-down kits that allowed stocks of all displayed items to be kept in store warehouses in flat pack boxes. Each of these practices resulted in economies that reinforced IKEA's position as the industry's low-price leader.[10]

4. IKEA used "humorous, off-beat advertising" to drive traffic to its stores, creating a vibe that attracted young, hip, urbanites, instead of appealing to the usual "older, more affluent consumers" (which was the standard target of furniture companies). IKEA had no fear in reaching out to and creating a new customer base and demographic. In some stores, as a result of their advertising approach, "650,000 visitors [were attracted] in its first year."[8]
5. IKEA's hiring practices were geared for corporate culture, not "busi-ness smarts":

   Because it had such a strong and unique culture, IKEA preferred not to recruit those who had already been immersed in another cultural stream.

Nor was higher education necessary or even advantageous in IKEA. [Many managers did not] have a college education. 'The Stockholm-raised, highly educated, status-oriented individuals often find it difficult to adjust to the culture of the company' remarked one executive. 'Younger, more open recruits not only keep costs low, but they also absorb and amplify the enthusiasm of the company.'[11]

How did Kamprad drive such initiatives and new ways of doing things? His leadership model was clear: "No method is more effective than the good example."[12]

LEADING BY MODELING

If IKEA was to represent frugality and Spartan living, then for Kamprad, the only way to drive buy-in for this cost-conscious strategy was for him to lead by example. Despite being one of the richest men in the world, worth $40 billion and having established the biggest furniture chain in the world, Kamprad maintains the simplest of lifestyles. At 90 years of age, he still drives his 13-year-old Volvo, takes public transit, and routinely flies economy. Says Kamprad, "I look at the money I'm about to spend on myself, and ask myself if IKEA customers can afford it."[13] This kind of thinking and behavior, given Kamprad's wealth, is as revolutionary as IKEA itself. No wonder IKEA has upended the furniture world. Kamprad models his own values and philosophies in a powerful and sacrificial manner. It doesn't get more credible than that. When people see Kamprad's commitment to the common person and his identification with the everyday worker, they are inspired. Kamprad has the means to live with the richest of them, but he chooses not to.

When you ask people to follow you in your mission of caring, what could be more powerful than your own example? Employees follow, fans flock, and IKEA changes the world because Kamprad breathes authenticity into the brand by living at the highest level of consistency between his life and what IKEA stands for.

BOOT CAMP #3: PERSONAL DEVELOPMENT

1. Why do people follow you? Name 2–3 key reasons why they do.

2. What are you doing to insure people will continue to follow you?

3. Growing your company involves growing yourself. Being disruptive means being disrupted yourself. How have you been disrupted in your career and how did that translate into how you lead?

Section II

Construction: Organizational Arena

Progression to Impact

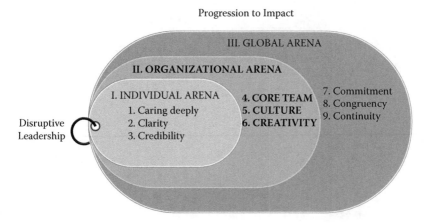

III. GLOBAL ARENA

II. ORGANIZATIONAL ARENA

I. INDIVIDUAL ARENA
1. Caring deeply
2. Clarity
3. Credibility

4. CORE TEAM
5. CULTURE
6. CREATIVITY

7. Commitment
8. Congruency
9. Continuity

Disruptive
Leadership

FIGURE S.II
Key chain.

5

Core Team: Finding Those Who Care Deeply with Me

David had his mighty men who gave him strong support in his kingdom—

I Chr. 11:11

To get where David was going, he needed his mighty men. There was no way David was going to reach the top and rule with distinction without a core team he could trust. History tells us that David had a cadre of mighty men who supported him in his cause,[1] but his inner circle consisted of three men who were particularly outstanding. The first, by the name of Adino, single-handedly killed 800 men with a spear in a heroic standoff. The second, Eleazar, battled an entire Philistine unit with such vigor that his hand froze to the handle of his sword. The third, Shammah, crazily, by himself, defended a plot of lentils, the company's food supply, by holding off a troop of invading Philistines. Each distinguished himself with acts of exceptional valor. As a team of three, they also broke into Bethlehem, the highly guarded Philistine-controlled garrison, to retrieve for David a cup of its renowned artesian water. That they risked their lives to satisfy David's craving for a refreshing drink he enjoyed as a boy showed how devoted and how much they loved their leader. David was surrounded by the best of the best and the most loyal of friends. For any leader looking to build a world-class organization, he must assemble a great core team. He must surround himself with "mighty men."

STEVE AND TEAM 1.0: THE APPLE TEAM (1976)

In our business, one person can't do anything anymore. You create a team of people around you.

—**Steve Jobs, Smithsonian Institution Oral and Video Histories, April 20, 1995**

Jobs has been called the Thomas Edison and Henry Ford of our time—an innovator that transcends boundaries and barriers.[2] Jobs, however, had lots of help along the way. Throughout his career, he continually surrounded himself, in various iterations, with the best—an inner circle of people who would march with him in their desire to achieve the remarkable. At Apple's inception in 1976, Team 1.0 was a mini-team of Steve and Steve, as in Steve Jobs and Steve Wozniak. The iconic duo was a picture of contrasts. If, as the saying goes, "opposites attract," then Jobs and Wozniak were a match made in opposite heaven.

While Jobs was the trailblazing visionary, Wozniak was the techno wunderkind. As a son of a Lockheed engineer, Wozniak cultivated his love of electronics by diving into the world of diodes and transistors, to the point of making his own calculator, microprocessor, and tone-based phone dialer.[3] He was the consummate tinkerer and extraordinarily good at it. Formally speaking, Wozniak was a double threat. He was a phenomenal hardware designer with keen engineering skills (employed at HP before starting Apple) who was also gifted at programming.[3] He could masterfully bring hardware and software together. As a result, there was an efficiency and integration baked into Apple's early computer creations that gave it a distinctly popular edge. So significant was Wozniak's work that Isaacson noted, "Wozniak deserves the historic credit for the design of its awe-inspiring circuit board and related operating software, which was one of the era's great feats of solo invention."[4] Later, in reflecting on Wozniak's contribution, Jobs shared, "Woz was somebody who was fifty times better than the average engineer. I wouldn't be here without his brilliance."[5]

If Wozniak was the wood from which a bonfire would be built, then Jobs was the gasoline and matchstick. Their skill sets did not overlap nor did their personality (Jobs never acquired any engineering or coding expertise). Jobs was bold and brash, while Wozniak was shy, even painfully so.

Jobs said, "Woz [was] very bright in some areas, but he [was] almost like a savant, since he was so stunted when it came to dealing with people he didn't know. We were a good pair."[6] Jobs loved to be out front, spreading the word and creating the buzz while Wozniak preferred being in the garage (literally) making things happen, as in putting together the first personal computer in history. In the age of IBM, mainframe computers, and COBOL, Apple's first creations—the Apple 1 in 1976 and Apple II in 1977—were a portend of its revolutionary vibe. That Jobs and Wozniak would pair up to do something so spectacular certainly could not have been predicted. Yet there was an unmistakable camaraderie that they had as Team 1.0. While the analogy is far from perfect, there was a Tom Sawyer–Huckleberry Finn-like quality to their relationship. Jobs, like Tom Sawyer, was the clever schemer with constant plans and plots running through in his head and able to make you, as Sawyer did, "pay for the privilege of painting fences." Wozniak, the Huckleberry Finn, was the likable follower, the modest and kinder one but also prone to occasional mischief (he was placed on probation at the University of Colorado Boulder for hacking into the university's computer system[7]). Though cut from different swaths, Tom Sawyer and Huckleberry Finn were inextricably linked together in adventure. So it was with Jobs and "Woz." As Wozniak would recount, Jobs' pitch for starting the company was not for the sake of money but camaraderie:

> "Even if we lose our money, we'll have a company," said Jobs as they were driving in his Volkswagen bus. "For once in our lives, we'll have a company." This was enticing to Wozniak, even more than any prospect of getting rich. He recalled, "I was excited to think about us like that. To be two best friends starting a company. Wow. I knew right then that I'd do it. How could I not?"[8]

So it was that Team 1.0 born in a VW bus. Not only did they care deeply about the road ahead, but there was also a care felt deeply between them.

At first, Wozniak wanted to keep the Apple I computer as a geeky kind of creation; one that other enthusiasts could enjoy. He stated, "I designed the Apple I because I wanted to give it away for free to other people."[9] But Jobs saw something bolder and grander, and convinced Wozniak that a personal computer was meant for the masses, not a niche group of technophiles. Convinced of its higher potential, the pair sped headlong toward making a computer desirable for the multitudes, not knowing that they would forever disrupt the computer industry. Though surrounded by other mentors in the early years—Regis McKenna (marketing), Mark Mukkala (strategy), Ron Wayne (venture funding)—it was this Team 1.0 that laid the foundation for things to come. They were the first to tilt the earth's axis.

STEVE AND TEAM 2.0: THE MACINTOSH TEAM (1984)

It's better to be a pirate than to join the Navy.[10]

—Steve Jobs

The introduction of Apple II in 1977, released just one year after Apple I, became a smashing success. In the first year of sales, the Apple II brought in $7.8 million of revenue and within two years surged to nearly $118 million in sales.[11] It was rocking the industry in a way never seen before and drawing the attention of national news outlets:

> No other company had ever grown that fast. The mainstream media began to take note, with publications like Esquire, Time, and Business Week starting serious coverage. Inc. went so far as to put Jobs on its cover, with the hosanna of a headline "This Man Has Changed Business Forever."[11]

So enduring was the Apple II that it "would be marketed, in various models, for the next sixteen years, with close to six million sold. More than any other machine, it launched the personal computer industry."[4] On the heels of its staggering success, Apple's valuation as a company rose from just over $5000 in January 1977 to nearly $1.8 *billion* in December 1980 when it went public. In the process, 300 people would become newly minted millionaires, and Jobs himself at the tender age of 25, would be worth $256 million.[12]

But on the heels of such success, the wheels of change were already turning. Team 1.0 was about to change into Team 2.0. Two events in particular converged to bring about the change. Jobs himself was already looking to the next big thing. Looking to build on the momentum of Apple II, Jobs was casting around for the next great computer configuration. Wozniak, however, was still absorbed in the Apple II and its improvements. Jobs was looking for the next revolution, while Wozniak was still working on the current one. Because of Wozniak's preoccupation with improving Apple II, other groups at Apple were experimenting with what the next quantum leap might look like. It turned out that a small group of four engineers led by Jef Raskin, a former professor at the University of California, San Diego, was working on a side project dubbed "Macintosh" (Raskin's favorite apple). Jobs became smitten with the project and, using his managerial might, mounted a hostile takeover.[13] It was an ugly and combative event, but Jobs prevailed and took over the team.[14] Wozniak's participation in the new emerging team, however, was not to be, as he had become medically impaired. In a near-fatal accident, Wozniak had developed amnesia after crashing his small private plane. Wozniak's absence, framed by the development of the Mac team, created a vacuum in which Jobs had to constitute a new team without Woz. (Indeed, after Wozniak recovered from his accident, he took a sabbatical from Apple, which ultimately led to Wozniak leaving Apple completely.[15]) Jobs thus forged ahead with what would become Team 2.0—the Macintosh team. Despite the loss of Woz, the shift proved invigorating to Jobs as he recalled, "It was like going back to the garage for me. I had my own ragtag team and I was in control."[14]

The initial core of the Macintosh team included the likes of Bill Atkinson, a graphics interface guru; Andy Hertzfeld, a gifted and tireless engineer; Burrell Smith, a world-class coder; and Joanna Hoffman, a feisty marketing executive who regularly stood up to Jobs. But the group quickly grew to 50-plus members, as Jobs went on a recruiting tear.[16]

> "The Macintosh is the future of Apple, and you're going to start on it now!" Jobs' primary test for recruiting people in the spring of 1981...was making sure they had a passion for the product. He would sometimes bring candidates into a room where a prototype of the Mac was covered by a cloth, dramatically unveil it, and watch. "If their eyes lit up, if they went right for the mouse and started pointing and clicking, Steve would smile and hire them. He wanted them to say 'Wow!'"[17]

It was during this crazy and frenetic season that Jobs created a new lexicon of sayings that would forever become associated with his genius. Jobs' ability to articulate, motivate, and thus recruit the best was a testament to his leadership ability and vision-casting power. Apple's success was to be built upon organizational excellence, which in turn was to be built upon the finest and most skilled people he could find. Jobs said, "I always considered part of my job was to keep the quality level of people in the organizations I work with very high. In everything I've done it really [paid] to go after the best people in the world."[18]

It was during the buildup of the Macintosh team that Jobs coined the now famous phrases of building "insanely great" products and "sending ripples through the universe." Anyone that joined the team would be "inventing the future" and making a "dent in the universe." And to cinch it all together, Jobs created a powerful team identity by referring to the group as pirates. As he told them at one of their famous team retreats, "It's better to be a pirate than join the navy." They would have a rebel identity. To be part of the establishment would be treason. In swashbuckling fashion they existed to take out the old order. So galvanized was the team by Jobs' vision that they took out a billboard ad to celebrate his 28th birthday. Read the sign along the road to Apple offices, "Happy 28th Steve. The Journey is the Reward—The Pirates." Team 2.0 had set sail with their leader, and the powerful Jobsian winds could not have been stronger or more exhilarating.[19]

STEVE AND TEAM 3.0: THE iTEAM (1997)

Despite the pursuit of insanely great products, Jobs, in hindsight, was becoming his worse management self and proved to be insanely impossible to work with. With the hypersonic growth of the company, Jobs had brought in "adult supervision" to fill the C-suites, notably John Sculley, the former head of PepsiCo, to assume the CEO role at Apple. While recruited by Jobs for his vaunted marketing reputation, Sculley soon found himself refereeing many of Jobs' skirmishes and managing the steady stream of complaints against Jobs' abrasive and bullying style. Jobs was often seen as petulant, repellent, and uncooperative. He was the classic "brilliant jerk not to be tolerated."[20] Jean-Louis Gassee, Apple's lead in France, even referred to Jobs as an "assaholic."[21] Jobs' over-the-top behavior, fueled by disappointing sales of the Macintosh (after its spectacular launch), finally boiled over. The board had to take action and, after several gut-wrenching months of meetings, decided Jobs had to leave. By the end of May 1985, Jobs was ousted from his own company.

Jobs was devastated and found himself rudderless for the first time in years. His humiliation was as spectacular as his rise. Yet Jobs found something undeniable inside. He was in a crucible but a purification was taking place. He would embrace his fall and learn from it. As he later put it,

> I didn't see it then, but it turned out that getting fired from Apple was the best thing that could have ever happened to me. The heaviness of being successful was replaced by the lightness of being a beginner again, less sure about everything. It freed me to enter one of the most creative periods of my life. During the next five years, I started a company named NeXT, [and] another company named Pixar. Pixar went on to create the world's first computer-animated feature film, *Toy Story*, and is now the most successful animation studio in the world. In a remarkable turn of events, Apple bought NeXT, I returned to Apple, and the technology we developed at NeXT is at the heart of Apple's current renaissance. I'm pretty sure none of this would have happened if I hadn't been fired from Apple. It was awful-tasting medicine, but I guess the patient needed it. Sometimes life hits you in the head with a brick. I'm convinced that the only thing that kept me going was that I loved what I did.[22]

Jobs' saving grace was knowing what he cared about. He could not have pulled through without it. He had become his own worst enemy, and it led to him being fired from one of Silicon Valley's great start-ups, his own nonetheless. Yet in his intervening "exile years" from Apple (1985–1997), through his start-ups at NeXT and Pixar, he would start over and build a new group, Team 3.0, that would eventually become the iTeam—the team that built the iMac, iPod, iPhone, and iPad. While at NeXT, he recruited Avadis Tevanian and Jonathan Rubenstein to be his software and hardware leads, respectively. They built a fancy, high-powered workstation for the educational market, but it failed in part because of its high price tag (over $6000 per machine) and lack of software applications. When Apple bought out NeXT as the basis of its future operating system (February 1997) and Jobs returned as CEO, Jobs quickly moved to install Tevanian and Rubenstein from NeXT as Apple's new software and hardware chiefs. Jobs would later appoint NeXT engineer Scott Forstall to be the mobile software lead of iOS. In time, Jobs' circle would be filled out by Jony Ive (design), Tim Cook (operations), Phil Schiller (marketing), Bob Mansfield (hardware), Eddy Cue (internet services), Ron Johnson (retail), and Peter Oppenheimer (finance).[23] This group would serve as Jobs' new mighty men, Team 3.0.

While Team 1.0 and Team 2.0 each made history, Team 3.0 inconceivably duplicated those feats and more. Each time Jobs had to pick himself up and dust himself off, he always returned to reconstituting a core team, finding those who would care deeply with him. This was a key for him in building a revolutionary company. There had to be a vested group that would be 110% committed and on fire to change the world. From there, the enthusiasm would radiate out to the rest of the company and then the world. In speaking of his role as team leader, he remarked, "I have one of the best jobs in the world. I'm incredibly lucky. I get to come into work every morning and hang around some of the most wonderful, brightest, committed, people I've ever met in my life. And together we get to play in the best sandbox I've ever seen and try to build great products for people."[24]

NAVY SEALS, RYDER CUP, AND THE RULE OF 4.6

Jobs' love for building crack teams applied to more than just the key people around him. It applied to the entire company. He loved to talk about how there were no committees at Apple. "We're organized like a start-up. We're the biggest start-up on the planet."[25] This is how Jobs would keep "hierarchy at bay"[26] and keep product ideas moving ahead quickly and efficiently (e.g., just two engineers wrote the code for the Safari browser on the iPad.[27]). Jobs believed "small groups composed of the smartest and most creative people had propelled Apple to its amazing success, and he had no intention of ever changing that."[28] Jobs loved the collaborative energy of people clustered in groups of three to ten.[27,29] And it turned out, his intuition was backed by research.

Navy SEALs (Sea, Air, Land) are known as the elite of the elite. They are the toughest and smartest troops in the military and part of the Navy's special operations forces. They are assigned to tackle only the most difficult of assignments (e.g., capturing or eliminating Al-Qaeda leader Osama bin Laden). Part of the secret behind their effectiveness is that platoons of SEALs are broken down into teams of four or five men, and they train, eat, and sleep together to build unity, cohesiveness, and brotherhood. They become so versed with each other that they understand one another instinctively and act as one man.

Separately, upon learning how the SEALs created high-performing teams, Paul Azinger, the 2008 U.S. Ryder Cup captain, wondered if the technique could work for the swooning U.S. team.[30] After three successive losses to the European side, the United States was desperate to get a win. Various attempts by the previous captains had not worked, and Azinger thought long and hard about how to create the proper chemistry for the U.S. contingent. Since the SEALs' training was a proven technique, Azinger decided to implement the pod concept where the 12-man U.S. team would be broken down into three teams of four players. Members for each team were chosen carefully to maximize unity, complement skills, and create brotherly bonds. The strategy worked perfectly as not only did the United States win back the Ryder Cup but they never trailed in any of the sessions against the Europeans. They won by the largest margin of victory since 1981. The SEALs' concept turned out to be just the powerful catalyst that the Ryder team had hoped for.

Much research has been done investigating the optimal size of teams, and it turns out five members has turned up consistently as the magic number:

> J. Richard Hackman, a professor of social and organizational psychology at Harvard, bans his students from forming project groups larger than six. Add just one more person, he writes in Leading Teams, "and the difference in how well groups of the two sizes operate is noticeable. In 1970, Hackman and Neil Vidmar (professor at University of Western Ontario) set out to find the perfect size. They asked teams large and small to do several tasks, then asked the participants how strongly they agreed with two statements: One, their group was too small for the task, and two, their group was too large. The optimum number: 4.6"[31]

Locating the best team size is a holy grail, and while context impacts what that number is, the concept of five or thereabouts is key, just as Jobs instinctively did with his inner core. And as history would have it, another leader (not far from Apple's California headquarters) was also creating a powerhouse team. An unsuspecting young man by the name of Phil Knight was building an athletic company never seen before for its influence and reach. As with Jobs, bringing together an inner core was crucial for Knight, except with Knight he did it with one enduring team for his career. The size of his team? Five.

CHASING AFTER RUNNING: NIKE

It's a struggle to find your dream, but when you find it, never let it go.[32]

—**Phil Knight, founder, Nike**

Nike is the largest athletic company in the world with sales of over $32 billion (2016). Its presence, as represented by its ubiquitous swoosh logo and superstar endorsers (e.g., Michael Jordan—basketball; Tiger Woods—golf; Cristiano Ronaldo—soccer; Rafael Nadal—tennis), has become such a force in culture that in 2015, it became the number one apparel brand in the world—not just the number one sports apparel brand but the number one brand in the entire apparel industry, beating the likes of Zara, H & M, Ralph Lauren, and Hugo Boss.[33] It owns more than 60% of the athletic shoe market in the United States[34] and over 30% globally.[35] It was founded in 1964 by Phil Knight when no one expected a skinny, young 26-year-old from Oregon to redefine the athletic shoe industry.

Knight's path to success is a story of self-awareness, honesty, and how an unassuming young man came to grips with what really mattered to him. Well-educated (University of Oregon undergrad degree in journalism, Stanford MBA)[36] but unfocused, Knight set off, after getting his degrees, on a round-the-world trip to get things clear in his head. Knight stated,

> Like all my friends I wanted to be successful. Unlike my friends I didn't know what that meant. Money? Maybe. Wife? Kids? House? Sure, if I was lucky. These were the goals I was taught to aspire to, and part of me did aspire to them, instinctively. But deep down I was searching for something else, something more. I had an aching sense that our time is short, shorter than we ever know, short as a morning run, and I wanted mine to be meaningful. And purposeful. And creative. And important. Above all... different. I wanted to leave a mark on the world.[37]

As Knight bounced around the world from Japan to Cairo to Milan and everywhere in between, he began sorting through his feelings and thoughts. Along the way, to make ends meet, he took up selling encyclopedias in Hawaii. It turned out to be a disastrous turn of events as his deep shyness kicked in and prevented him from landing any sales. It didn't help that he was reading *Catcher in the Rye*, where he identified deeply with Holden

Caulfield's sense of insecurity as "the teenage introvert seeking his place in the world."[38] As Knight recounted of the dreadful experience,

> I couldn't sell encyclopedias to save my life... The sight of my extreme discomfort often made strangers uncomfortable. Thus, selling anything would have been challenging, but selling encyclopedias, which were about as popular in Hawaii as mosquitoes and mainlanders, was an ordeal. No matter how deftly or forcefully I managed to deliver the key phrases drilled into us during our brief training session... I always got the same response. Beat it, kid.[39]

Digging deeper, Knight would share,

> If my shyness made me bad at selling encyclopedias, my nature made me despise it. I wasn't built for heavy doses of rejection. I'd known this about myself since high school, freshman year, when I got cut from the baseball team. A small setback, in the grand scheme, but it knocked me sideways. It was my first real awareness that not everyone in this world will like us, or accept us, that we're often cast aside at the very moment we most need to be included. I will never forget that day. Dragging my bat along the sidewalk, I staggered home and holed up in my room, where I grieved, and moped, for about two weeks.[40]

But as can happen in life, our biggest defeats turn into our greatest opportunities. Knight's mother stepped in to comfort him at that time, which in hindsight became the foundation for why Knight started Nike:

> My mother appeared on the edge of my bed and said, "Enough." She urged me to try something else. "Like what?" I groaned into my pillow. "How about track?" she said. "Track?" I said. "You can run fast." "I can?" I said, sitting up. So I went out for track. And I found that I could run. And no one could take that away. [41]

Knight could run indeed, and he ran well enough to compete at the Division 1 level at the University of Oregon. His best time in the mile was a respectable four minutes and ten seconds. But as Knight would state, that was as far as he would go:

> I'd run track at Oregon, and I'd distinguished myself, lettering three of four years. But that was that, the end. At different times I'd fantasized about becoming a great novelist, a great journalist, a great statesman. But the

ultimate dream was always to be a great athlete. Sadly, fate had made me good, not great.[42]

Although Knight would never have a career as a professional athlete, running became his passion, a way to recharge amidst the beautiful Oregon scenery where he grew up.

What a beautiful place to be from, I thought, gazing around. Calm, green, tranquil—I was proud to call Oregon my home, proud to call little Portland my place of birth.[43]

But Oregon did not just give Knight a sense of place. It would give Knight a big dose of the pioneering spirit the first settlers had when they made their way out west. As one of his childhood teachers taught him, the original Oregonians were famous for the trails they blazed, and it was the new Oregonians' responsibility to keep that strain of pioneering spirit alive. For Knight, entrepreneurs would be the new breed of pioneers.

While enjoying the Oregon trails, it all became clear: running was not a hobby, it was his love. Running was what gave Knight joy. Driven by shyness and rejection, he got into running on his mom's advice, but it turned out to be not just a comforting alternative but a game-changing moment. As Knight would state, "My favorite thing [was] running."[44]

Running became Knight's unifying thought. This is how he would make his mark. And he would adopt the pioneering spirit of Oregon to accomplish it. As Knight recounted,

What if there were a way, without being an athlete, to feel what athletes feel? To play all the time, instead of working? Or else to enjoy work so much that it becomes essentially the same thing. The world was so overrun with war and pain and misery, the daily grind was so exhausting and often unjust— maybe the only answer, I thought, was to find some prodigious, improbable dream that seemed worthy, that seemed fun, that seemed a good fit, and chase it with an athlete's single-minded dedication and purpose.[45]

These were the thoughts rushing through Knight's mind as he traveled the world. Although advertised to his dad as a trip to find himself, it was actually a cover for Knight to make a side trip to Japan and find out whether a paper he wrote for his Stanford MBA entrepreneurship class was just a crazy idea to be dispensed with or a crazy idea to start something big. While at the University of Oregon, Knight had become close friends with track coach Bill Bowerman who had a passion for tinkering with running shoes. Bowerman had trained 31 Olympians and 22 NCAA champions during his career and was obsessed with trying new kinds of shoe configurations to create faster running times (most famously popularized by his "waffle sole" design). Later, Knight would take those ideas to Stanford and made the argument that just as "Japanese cameras had made deep cuts into the camera market, which had once been dominated by Germans," so a similar thing could happen with the running shoe market.[46] Japan could be a great source of low-cost, high-quality athletic shoes. Knight got an "A" for his paper, but it stirred no excitement among his classmates or professor. The idea, however, stuck strongly with Knight, and he had to scratch his itch. Could his passion for running and shoe design translate into a mission? It turned out with some moxie Knight was able to follow through on his paper's action plan; he landed a contract to sell Onitsuka Tiger shoes in the States. Knight might have had a shyness issue, but given the opportunity to pursue his dream, no obstacles seemed too big. From Tokyo, he cold-called the Tiger company in Kobe and actually landed a meeting with the executives. Humorously, as he went into the meeting the next day, he had forgotten to identify the company he represented, so he had to make up one during introductions:

> "Mr. Knight—what company are you with?" "Ah, yes, good question." Adrenaline surging through my blood, I felt the flight response... "Blue Ribbon," I blurted. "Gentlemen, I represent Blue Ribbon Sports of Portland, Oregon."[47]

Knight had named his company after the many blue ribbons he had won while competing, and in a moment of quick-thinking, his dream of changing the running world took its first step.

Upon returning to the States, Knight shared what happened with his former coach. Bowerman was so impressed he asked to invest in the new company. Putting in $500 and matched by Knight, the $1000 became the seed money for what would become Nike. Bowerman, however, wanted no operational responsibilities.[48] Knight would have to build his own team.

―――――――――

KNIGHT AND HIS BUTTFACES

We did it together. That's kinda what the book is about.[49]

―Phil Knight on his biography and years at Nike

When Nike was formed (first called Blue Ribbon Sports from 1964–1971), Knight did not have an inner circle in place. Bowerman would serve as a strategist, father figure, and sounding board but not as a day-to-day executive. Knight would need to recruit others. The process was slow and arduous, but when Knight's team finally came together in 1976, they came together like super glue. Ironically, their identity was solidified by an insult. Jeff Johnson, Nike's first employee, was the instigator. Recalls Knight,

> Johnson coined the phrase, we think. At one of our earliest retreats he muttered: "How many multimillion-dollar companies can you yell out, 'Hey, Buttface,' and the entire management team turns around?" It got a laugh. And then it stuck. And then it became a key part of our vernacular. Buttface referred to both the retreat and the retreaters, and it not only captured the informal mood of those retreats, where no idea was too sacred to be mocked, and no person was too important to be ridiculed, it also summed up the company spirit, mission and ethos.[50]

It was a crystallizing moment. Just as Jobs had his pirates, so Knight would have his "we're-going-to-change-the-world" team, and they were called "Buttfaces." The team of five, a band of brothers as Knight would refer to them, was a mix of early employees and highly talented consultants that Knight had recruited. The depth of their camaraderie was measured by the abuse they could hurl at each other. The more abuse they could dish out, the more it was a sign of love and closeness. Each member had a nickname.

Jeff Johnson, employee number one, was a fellow Stanford student with Knight and a social worker before he joined Nike. He was tasked with opening the company's factory on the East Coast and developed the company's first line of running shoes using a special rubber found in teddy bears.[51] Johnson also had the distinction of coming up with "Nike" as the name to replace Blue Ribbon Sports. Because he was given to exaggeration, he was called "Four Factor" as in discount anything he said by four.

Bob Woodell, employee number four, was a long-jumper at the University of Oregon, and a day after helping his team win the 1966 NCAA track and field title, became paralyzed in a boating accident.[52] He excelled at operations and eventually became the company's first COO. He was cruelly or lovingly called "Dead Weight."

Delbert Hayes, originally from Price Waterhouse, became the company's accountant and eventual executive vice president (1980–1995). He was a whiz with numbers and had an uncanny ability to predict the future when given a spreadsheet. He was loud, flamboyant, and, as Knight would describe him, "morbidly obese." He was "six foot two, three hundred pounds, most of it stuff sausage—like into an exceedingly inexpensive polyester suit."[53] He was called "Doomsday," a name befitting a numbers guy.

Rob Strasser, a razor-sharp lawyer, and hired away by Knight from his local law firm, was considered by Knight as "one of the greatest thinkers I ever met. Debater, negotiator, talker, seeker—his mind was always whirring, trying to understand. And to conquer. Strasser was our five-star general, and I was ready to follow him into any fray, any fusillade."[54] Strasser became head of marketing at Nike and chief deal-maker. His most famous accomplishment was signing Michael Jordan, which to date has brought in $2.6 billion of revenue for the company from the Air Jordan line. It was a signature deal that shook up the industry and disrupted what was previously thought possible in elevating brand recognition with a star endorser.[55] Like Hayes, Strasser was physically huge. When Knight met Strasser for the first time, he was stunned. "I saw the rough contours of a man. Six-three, 280 pounds, with an extra helping of shoulders. And fire-log arms. This was one part Sasquatch, one part Snuffleupagus, though somehow light on his feet."[56] He was called "Rolling Thunder" for his outsized presence.

Of course, rounding out the band of brothers was Knight himself. Though the leader, he was not above the antics of the group. Indeed, it was special to be in the thick of it:

> Oh, what abuse. We called each other terrible names. We rained down verbal blows. While floating ideas, and shooting down ideas, and hashing out threats to the company, the last thing we took into account was someone's feelings. Including mine. Especially mine. My fellow Buttfaces,

my employees, called me Bucky the Bookkeeper, constantly. I never asked them to stop. I knew better. If you showed any weakness, any sentimentality, you were dead.[57]

And at the end of the day, Knight felt deeply blessed for the team that surrounded him:

> I [could] see myself so clearly at the head of a conference table, shouting, being shouted at—laughing until my voice was gone. The problems confronting us were grave, complex, seemingly insurmountable... And yet we were always laughing. Sometimes, after a really cathartic guffaw, I'd look around the table and feel overcome by emotion. Camaraderie, loyalty, gratitude. Even love. Surely love. But I also remember feeling shocked that these were the men I'd assembled. These were the founding fathers of a multimillion-dollar company that sold athletic shoes? A paralyzed guy, two morbidly obese guys, [and] a chain-smoking guy?[58]

This unlikely crew may not have mirrored the gleaming stable of stars that Nike was so famously known for, but they were mighty men in their own right and they gave Knight "strong support in his kingdom." And as the press release to Knight's book would describe, "Together, harnessing the transcendent power of a shared mission, and a deep belief in the spirit of sport, they built a brand that changed everything."[59] When you find those who care deeply with you, anything is possible.

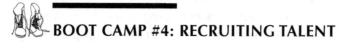 **BOOT CAMP #4: RECRUITING TALENT**

1. Who is on your core team right now? Name them.

2. Do each of them care as deeply as you want them to? If not, will you fire them or try to improve them?

3. Finding great talent is one of the most difficult tasks in building a world-class organization. What keys would you pass on to others to attract the best?

6

Culture: If You Don't Care, You Don't Belong

Culture is the #1 metric.[1]

—Gaping Void Consultancy

Culture is the soil of a company. Culture is the air you breathe and the ground you stand on. It's the foundation of a company as well as its secret ingredient. It's how people are nurtured to do great and impossible things. Formally speaking, culture has been variously defined as the "deeply held beliefs, attitudes, and values"[2] of an organization, "a clear set of values nd norms that actively guide the way a company operates,"[3] or "the way things get done around here."[4] The culture of a company is its identity and personality. The more disruptive a company is, the more potent its culture. And few companies have as potent a culture as Apple.

As improbable as it may seem, it is easier to get admitted to Harvard than it is getting a job at Apple. While Harvard's admission rate is a measly 7%, there is only a paltry 2% chance to get a job at, say, Apple's Manhattan store where only 200 out of 10,000 applicants get accepted.[5] Why such a stampede? Because Apple's culture of caring deeply acts like a super magnet. Everyone wants to be part of it. If the number one metric of an organization is culture (as many experts now espouse), then Apple is certainly the leader of the pack as demonstrated by those wanting to sport the Apple logo on their work badge.

WHY APPLE'S CULTURE IS SO ATTRACTIVE

What makes Apple's culture so alluring and magnetic? How did Apple become such a force of nature? Edgar Schein, the father of organizational culture, breaks down culture into three levels: (1) artifacts of an organization—the visible and tangible attributes of the company; (2) values and norms—the company's operating principles and ideals; and (3) foundational assumptions—which undergird the organization's values and aspirations.[6] When filtered through Schein's model, it becomes clear why Apple possesses such might.

MESMERIZING "ARTIFACTS"

The first thing that makes Apple's culture so powerful is the visible manifestations of the company.[7] The romance and love affair that people all over world have with Apple products is unprecedented. The iPod took a moribund mp3 industry by storm in 2001 and by 2014 had sold 390 million total units.[8] The iPhone introduced in 2007 overturned the smartphone industry and knocked out market leaders Nokia, Motorola, and Blackberry.[9] As of 2016, 1 *billion* iPhones had been sold, making it the most successful consumer product in history.[10] The iPhone has been so disruptive that Finland (home of Nokia) blamed Apple for damaging its national economy.[11] Canada's Blackberry, once the hottest phone on the planet, was so blindsided by iPhone's success that, it exited the market altogether in 2016.[12] The iPad came out in 2010 and became the fastest selling product in Apple's history, selling 84 million units and claiming 94% usage by Fortune 500 companies within two years.[7] People line up for days to get their hands on Apple's latest products (YouTube videos abound), providing a powerful testament to Apple's amazing "artifacts."

To showcase Apple's products, Steve Jobs also revolutionized the retail industry with the company's own store concept. Jobs did not want "an iMac to sit on a shelf between a Dell and a Compaq."[13] He wanted to have people's undivided attention and a way to directly "communicate to

[the] customer." As Ron Johnson, Apple's first chief of retail, stated, "The store will become the most powerful physical expression of the brand."[14]

Nothing was spared to create the most engaging and immersive environment. For example, Pietra Serena sandstone from Florence, Italy, was specially imported to adorn the store's floors. While it would have saved a lot of money to create an imitation texture of the stone using concrete, Jobs wanted the floor to be authentic. He loved and insisted that the gray stone color be the real thing.[15] When Apple was building its iconic New York Fifth Avenue store, Jobs was so vested in building a gorgeous glass cube entrance that he himself paid $9 million to have it built and became the structure's owner. The care that Jobs and the Apple team put into the stores paid off handsomely, as they would become the most profitable retail space in the world, bringing in an eye-popping $4800 per square foot, far outdistancing second place Tiffany's ($3100 per square foot) and lapping third place Michael Kors ($1900 per square foot).[16] Apple's store became exactly what Johnson had predicted, "the most powerful expression of the brand." The physical beauty and warmth of the stores sealed the bond between consumers and Apple's culture.

Apple's mesmerizing artifacts were also manifest in their ad campaigns— print, TV, and video. Their 1984 Super Bowl ad became a landmark event. It was released to promote the introduction of the Macintosh and featured an Orwellian theme of Apple pitted against oppressive Big Brothers of the day (Goliaths). So stunning and stark was the 60-second advertisement that Advertising Age named it the greatest commercial of all time.[17] Apple's iPod print ads that featured the product's signature white earbuds against solid color backgrounds became another example of Apple's iconic approach. And their video shorts of "I'm a PC versus I'm a Mac" featuring a pudgy, geeky-looking John Hodgman (Microsoft), up against the cool, hipster Justin Long (Apple) imprinted in people's minds the vast difference between Macs and non-Macs.

All this served to deeply capture people's imagination. From Apple's gorgeously designed website to their airy, welcoming stores, to owning their products, everything about Apple drew people in. Never had a company developed such an impressive array of artifacts. But that was just the "external manifestations" of Apple's genius. To understand Apple's culture more fully, one needs to further consider its deeper, governing principles.

MANIACAL MINDSETS: WASHING MACHINES, BOOT TIMES, AND COLOR PALETTES

How does Apple pull off such breathtaking feats time after time? It's all rooted in their desire to make human-centered products with uncompromising standards. One particular story illustrates the kind of maniacal attention Jobs would give to a product, and in this case, not even one related to Apple. At one point, the Jobs' family needed a new washer and dryer. Typically, this would be a routine weekend buying event; make a checklist of desired features, match it against the budget, select the product, and have it delivered. But for Jobs and the family, it became a tortured two-week discussion:

> We spent some time in our family talking about what's the trade-off we want[ed] to make. We ended up talking a lot about design, but also about the values of our family. Did we care most about getting our wash done in an hour versus an hour and a half? Or did we care most about our clothes feeling really soft and lasting longer? Did we care about using a quarter of the water? The discussion revolved around American versus European design, the amount of water and detergent consumed, the speed of the wash, and the longevity of the clothes. In the end, Jobs opted for German appliances. These guys really thought the process through. They did such a great job designing these washers and dryers. I got more thrill out of them than I have out of any piece of high tech in years.[18]

Such deliberation and thoughtfulness serves to illustrate that Jobs' commitment to making the best products in the world was not a job or vocation but a love. It was how Jobs was wired. The way he lived and contemplated things in his personal life is how he led product design at Apple. His mindset was the company's.

In another instance, during the development of the Mac's operating system, Jobs felt the boot-up time was too long and wanted it reduced by 10 seconds. Larry Kenyon, the engineer working on it, didn't think it was that necessary until Jobs launched into a passionate user-centered argument.

> "If it could save a person's life, would you find a way to shave ten seconds off the boot time?" he asked. Kenyon allowed that he probably would. Jobs went to a whiteboard and showed that if there were five million people using the

Mac and it took ten seconds extra to turn it on every day, that added up to three hundred million or so hours per year that people would save, which was the equivalent of at least one hundred lifetimes saved per year. "Larry was suitably impressed, and a few weeks later he came back and it booted up twenty-eight seconds faster." Steve had a way of motivating by looking at the bigger picture. The result was that the Macintosh team came to share Jobs' passion for making a great product, not just a profitable one. The goal was never to beat the competition, or to make a lot of money. It was to do the greatest thing possible, or even a little greater.[19]

Underscoring Apple's commitment to even the smallest detail, no company had mastered and majored on the power of color like Apple had. When the Apple II was introduced, Jobs went through more than two thousand shades of beige before settling on the right one.[20] Then several years later when he discerned beige had become passé, he introduced the iMac with colors such as Biondi blue, tangerine, ruby, and sage. It was bold and different, but more than just trying to be novel, it was designed to capture an affinity and affection people had for color they didn't know they had. To this day, the effort Apple puts into the color and tactile feel of its products is unparalleled. When they released the iPhone 7, they innovated a whole new process to achieve the high-gloss finish associated with their jet-black color option. The process includes rotational 3D polishing, anodization, single-dye absorption, and a magnetized ion bath. What company does this? What company exerts this kind of effort to get the color and finish right? On the other hand, what company has a culture that is so compelling?

And then there is the matter of Apple's penchant for secrecy, so fierce it's said to rival operations at the CIA (and maybe Fort Knox combined). What was inside the psyche of Jobs that insisted on a cone of silence on all projects until the day they were unveiled, impacting even how employees could talk (or not talk) to each other (which has been noted as one of the objectionable aspects of the company's culture). Dr. Gary Chapman has written a fascinating book called *The 5 Love Languages* in which he describes how people give and receive love through one of five ways—quality time, words of affirmation, acts of service, physical touch, or gift giving.[21] If this teaching were applied to Apple as a person, it's clear Apple's love language would be gift giving. Something in Jobs understood the power of gifts—not only the gift itself but the presenting of gifts and the feeling of being surprised with something wonderfully elegant and pure. Jobs' commitment to secrecy was actually a commitment to delighting, and secrecy and surprise was a way to intensify delight to its highest levels. Jobs was a master at identifying the human experience and committing to it.

Jobs' leadership and his way of looking at things inculcated something deep within Apple. While the mesmerizing artifacts were the most tangible evidence of Apple's work, it was this underlying mindset that gave rise to Apple's great popularity and imparted inestimable vigor to its culture. Then, there is the company's bedrock layer.

A MISSION OF MAGNITUDE: LEAVE A CRATER

On May 25, 2016, Donovan Livingston, graduating from Harvard with a Master's degree in Education, was chosen to address his fellow classmates in a commencement speech. What followed was an electrifying spoken word presentation that was hailed as one of the greatest student graduation speeches ever given.[22] Harvard itself stated it was "one of the most powerful speeches you'll ever hear." In the midst of his soaring oratory about racial inequality within the educational systems, Livingston touched on mission, purpose, and potential that could have easily been a refrain of Jobs' aspiration to "put a dent in the universe." Livingston stated,

> At the core, none of us were meant to be common.
> We were born to be comets,
> Darting across space and time—
> Leaving our mark as we crash into everything.
> A crater is a reminder that something amazing happened here—
> An indelible impact that shook up the world.[23]

Livingston's credo? Our lives were created to be powerful, meaningful, and disruptive. Dare it be said, Jobs would have heartily applauded the young man's remarks. "Leaving our mark as we crash into everything. A crater is a reminder that something amazing happened here." That is a manifesto to care deeply about what you do with your life. It also bears the voice of a transformational leader. One who will point the way and create a place to which people want to belong and participate in. That voice creates the highest kind of culture—a place where purpose prevails over profit and meaning prevails over money. This kind of vision to change the world is what animated Jobs. It's what sat at the center of Apple's culture. If you don't care, then you don't belong. This foundational principle reflects Schein's final and deepest level of culture—i.e., the reason a company exists and what are its nonnegotiables. For Apple, people flock to work for the company because of what it stands for in its products, its values, and its mission. When those three align in perfect harmony, you build a culture that sings.

To build a great company, you must build a great culture. That culture in turn becomes your tool for creating momentum, making impact, and attracting the best people. The exciting part of establishing great corporate cultures is it works in any kind of business or industry. And a young man by the name of Tony Hsieh proved that to great effect by creating a zany, upbeat culture in the shoe industry doing something no one thought possible—selling shoes online.

SHAKING UP THE ONLINE SHOE LANDSCAPE: ZAPPOS

In 1999, when Zappos founder Nick Swinmurn couldn't find the shoes he liked at a local San Francisco mall, he thought he could source it online. To his frustration, he found he couldn't find it there either. So, he decided to do something about it. Cheekily, he quit his day job and decided to launch an online shoe company.[24] Needing start-up money and some business smarts on his side, he approached Tony Hsieh for help. Hsieh had just completed the sale of his company LinkExchange to Microsoft for $265 million and had started an investment firm called Venture Frog. While first dismissive of selling shoes unseen to customers, the size of the $40 billion shoe market caught Hsieh's attention. Upon hearing that 5% of the market was already being sold through online catalogs, it was enough to convince Hsieh that an online retail concept was worth a try. After a $500,000 investment, Zappos got started and a few months later, Hsieh joined Swinmurn as co-CEO. Within a year, the company realized $1.6 million in sales, and by its fifth year, sales had soared to $184 million. By 2008, the company reached $1 billion in revenue, which turned out to be two years ahead of its ambitious goals. By then, Zappos had established itself as the market leader and champion of the online space for shoes. They had done what no one thought possible. In 2009, Fortune Magazine named Zappos as one of the top 25 companies to work for. In less than ten years, they went from nobody to revolutionary.

IT'S NOT ABOUT SHOES

How did Zappos achieve its success? How did they get people to buy shoes without trying them on or "testing driving" them in traditional brick and mortar stores? The answer is Zappos does not see itself in the shoe business. Hsieh states, "Back in 2003, we thought of ourselves as a shoe company that offered great service. Today, we really think of the Zappos brand as about great service, and we just happen to sell shoes."[25] Hsieh's thinking process went like this, "We asked ourselves what we wanted this company to stand for. We didn't want to sell just shoes. I wasn't even into shoes—I used to wear a pair with holes in them—but I was passionate about customer service. I wanted us to have a whole company built around it."[26]

As referred to in Chapter 3, disruptive companies derive their energy from higher values. Just as Danny Meyer stated his restaurants were not about great food but creating a memorable hospitality experience, Hsieh stated Zappos' secret was not in shoes but in a fanatical commitment to service. His goal was "not just satisfying customers, but amazing them."[27]

Stories abound of extreme acts of customer care at Zappos. In one case, "Zappos sent flowers to a woman who ordered six different pairs of shoes because her feet were damaged by harsh medical treatments."[28] In another, "a customer service rep physically went to a rival shoe store to get a specific pair of shoes for a woman staying at the Mandalay Bay hotel in Vegas when Zappos ran out of stock."[28] And again, Zappos agents have helped customers research competitor's website to find what they need. Zappos shook up the industry by providing services never previously offered, like two-way free shipping (to the customer and for returns), and a 365-day return policy (for shoes!).[29] And to insure customer calls are handled with genuine, spontaneous interaction, Zappos prohibits the use of scripts.[28] No wonder the company's byline is "Powered by Service."

HIRING TO CULTURE

How does Zappos create an army of people deeply committed to serving the client?

> In an age of clueless, surly or impossible-to-reach customer service personnel, Zappos's fanaticism helps it stand out. *It is all in the hiring.* After a few weeks of intensive training, new call-center employees are offered $1,000 on top of what they have earned to that point if they want to quit. The theory... is that the people who take the money obviously don't have the sense of commitment Zappos requires from its employees. The company says 10% of its trainees take the offer.[27]

The idea of paying people to quit was a crazy idea (and made waves in the industry when Zappos introduced it), but it fit perfectly into the cultural scheme Zappos was setting for recruiting only enthusiastic, people-focused employees. Hsieh stated, "We want people who are passionate about what Zappos is about—service. I don't care if they're passionate about shoes."[30] This kind of hiring represented a new kind of strategy. With culture as the primary filter, Zappos was utilizing a tribal mechanism for building greatness. Hsieh goes on,

> At Zappos, culture is the number one priority for the company. We do two sets of interviews for everyone we hire. The hiring managers interview for the standard stuff like relevant experience, technical ability, and the HR department does a second interview for culture fit. Candidates have to pass both to be hired. We've actually passed on a lot of smart, talented people we know can make an immediate impact on our top and bottom line, but if they're not good for our culture, we won't hire them.[31]

GOING TRIBAL

The idea of "going tribal" is the notion that to belong to "our" organization, you must not just fit here; you must fit into this tribe. There has to be a gut-level, high-powered affinity from us to you and you to us. This gut-level, high-powered affinity is based on the culture and values of the organization, i.e., how we think, act, work, and play. If there is not a cultural fit, that dynamic magical "I'm all in" feeling, then you can't wear the war paint and carry the spears with us. If you don't care like us, you don't belong with us.

In addition to the cultural fit interviews, Zappos employs a final "kindness test." It's a "shuttle bus" check that goes like this:

> A lot of our candidates are from out of town, and we'll pick them up from the airport in a Zappos shuttle, give them a tour, and then they'll spend the rest of the day interviewing. At the end of the day of interviews, the recruiter will circle back to the shuttle driver and ask how he or she was treated. It doesn't matter how well the day of interviews went, if our shuttle driver wasn't treated well, then we won't hire that person.[32]

This is screening for hires at the deepest value levels of the company and shows how Zappos has created incredible alignment between their culture and hiring. For Zappos, being kind is a nonnegotiable and in the end an automatic veto for hiring if one is unkind. It's a radical approach. But if you can imagine a company full of kind people manning the phones as they talk about shoe orders, then you understand why Zappos has turned their industry upside down and become the most successful online shoe retailer in the country. This culture stuff works.

Needless to say, with such zeal for company culture, firing is also based on culture. If an employee turns out to be a nonfit, they are let go. Hsieh is as clear about how someone is fired as how they are hired.[31] Because the company's culture is central to the success of the company, firing is seen as a necessary part of protecting and maintaining the essential integrity of the organization.[33]

DELIVERING HAPPINESS

More recently, in its ongoing evolution of creating a cultural powerhouse, Hsieh has begun to espouse the concept of delivering happiness, and elevating each employee's experience to yet another level of enjoyment. By helping employees connect personal happiness with their work life,

Hsieh is looking to create a joy-filled and contented lot of workers; those who see Zappos not just as their work, but as part of their happiness lifestyle. According to Zappos, "companies with a higher sense of purpose outperform those without by 400%." Various studies show that when a company possesses a higher purpose, they achieve the following:[34]

300% more innovation (HBR)
44% higher retention (Gallup)
37% increase in sales (Shawn Anchor)
31% increase in productivity (Shawn Anchor)
125% less burnout (HBR)
66% fewer sick leaves (Forbes)
51% less turnover (Gallup)

All this makes for companies in which impact, disruption, and leadership are the norm. Apple has proven this. Zappos has proven this. And any company willing to build organizations with fantastic cultures can add their name to the list as well. And like Apple and Zappos, they will soon find the world beating a path to their door. For culture, it's go big or go home.

BOOT CAMP #5: CORE VALUES

1. You build your company's culture through your core values. What are they? Write them down.

2. Is it clear in your mind how you will translate these values into your organization's culture? Think deeply about this. Bring in others on this conversation. Refer back to this chapter how Apple and Zappos accomplished this.

3. Have you seen your organization's culture as a value-added advantage over industry peers? Have you seen it as a weapon of disruption? If not, upgrade your thinking so you can harness its power. Make an argument to yourself why this is true. Write it down here.

7

Creativity: Caring Leads to Crazy, Delightful Solutions

Being the richest man in the cemetery doesn't matter to me. Going to bed at night saying we've done something wonderful... that's what matters to me.[1]

—Steve Jobs to billionaire Larry Ellison, founder of Oracle

MEASURING WONDERFUL

Even though Apple is the most valuable company in the world[2] and possesses the most valuable brand in the world six years running,[3] what delights Apple is delighting the customer. And as indicated by the customer loyalty, they seem to be doing just that. Recent surveys have shown 99% customer satisfaction with the iPhone 6S and 6S Plus and 97% satisfaction for iPad Air 2.[4] According to Morgan Stanley, "Apple has a 90 percent brand retention rate"[5] and "iPhone users are more loyal to Apple than users of any other smartphone brand are."[6] As noted by Betanews, "Apple has brand loyalty that most companies can only dream of,"[5] and as succinctly put by Harvard Business Review's Horace Dediu, "The number one message about Apple is it is a loyalty story."[7]

NO INSTRUCTIONS INCLUDED

How has Apple come to this wonderful perch of "wonderfulness?" How has it created such an army of loyalists? Apple has many competitors doing the same thing, trying to make great computers, smartphones, tablets, and watches, and yet no company elicits the fierce kind of loyalty that Apple has. Why has this happened and how has Apple achieved a different level of success? In a word, Apple's "X" factor is its creativity. No company has so disrupted the world with its creativity like Apple has.

When the iMac was shipped, one of the most amazing things about it was that no instructions were included. Apple believed its computer was so simple and intuitive, customers would not need a user's manual. They could just noodle around, and by golly, they'd get it. Apple's commitment to elegant simplicity led to arguably, the "no-instructions-needed" revolution. Never before had this been done. Apple hoisted the industry on its shoulders and carried it to a completely different place. Rather than getting people to conform to technology (remember: C:\>del or C:\>edit?), they made technology conform to the people. Jobs stated it this way:

> One of the things I've always found is that you've got to start with the customer experience and work backwards for the technology. You can't start with the technology and try to figure out where you're going to try to sell it. As we have tried to come up with a strategy and a vision for Apple, it started with "What incredible benefits can we give to the customer? Where can we take the customer?" Not starting with "Let's sit down with the engineers and figure out what awesome technology we have and then how are we going to market that?" And I think that's the right path to take.[8]

Apple's approach toward creativity was something new and powerful. It was about technology being humanized rather than human beings mechanized. To make something truly wonderful, it had to be truly personal. By turning convention on its head, Apple flipped the starting point of design. Instead of beginning with the specs, they began with the person. This mindset revolutionized the tech space and unleashed a series of innovations never seen before.

WORKING BACKWARD IS THE WAY TO LEAP FORWARD

In his relentless pursuit of wedding beauty with technology, Jobs was introduced to a new graphical user interface (GUI) invented by Xerox at its Palo Alto Research Center (PARC) and conceived by visionary scientist Alan Kay. Kay envisioned a computer so simple that children could use it. To do that, he had to create a new kind of interactive medium that would "replace all the command lines and DOS prompts that made computer screens intimidating."[9] In its place, Xerox engineers came up with an icon-based system in which the screen was now seen as a desktop, and it would have "many documents and folders on it, and you could use a mouse to point and click on the one you wanted to use."[9] The screen would be animated by objects that looked like folders and files because Xerox scientists devised a way to bitmap the entire screen. This meant the processor controlled every pixel on the screen and could thus create life-like images instead of being limited to using just characters. By being able to turn every pixel on or off, graphical images could replace the character-based environment of the current DOS-dominated computers. It was like going from a text-only book to a picture book. It was a game changer. When Jobs saw the Xerox PARC interface, he flipped. While Xerox's engineers saw their operating system in a research kind of way with future benefits, Jobs saw something revolutionary right then and there. So excited was Jobs, he was said to have "bounced around and waved his arms excitedly."[10] Said one of the Xerox scientists,

> He was hopping around so much I don't know how he actually saw most of the demo, but he did, because he kept asking questions. He was the exclamation point for every step I showed. Jobs kept saying that he couldn't believe that Xerox had not commercialized the technology. "You're sitting on a gold mine," he shouted. "I can't believe Xerox is not taking advantage of this....This is it! We've got to do it!" It was the breakthrough he had been looking for: bringing computers to the people, with the cheerful but affordable design of an Eichler home and the ease of use of a sleek kitchen appliance."[9]

In hindsight, what Kay had done with his team was to mimic the very design aesthetic that Jobs was so passionate about. By creating the GUI with children in mind, they had inherently made it user friendly and human centered. It was a living incarnation of Jobs' values in computer form. The moment he saw it, he knew this was "it." Indeed, the Xerox interface became the new system architecture of the Mac, and as has been noted by historians, represented "one of the biggest heists in the chronicles of the industry."[11] The Mac would go on to make history, but that moment validated Jobs' passion for user-centric products. The genie was out of the bottle. There was no turning back. Leap frogging ahead was about reaching back and connecting with the customer. Or as Alan Kay put it, "The best way to predict the future is to invent it."[9]

As a result Apple would go on, over and over again, to pioneer fresh ways to interact with technology. Indeed, Apple continued their disruptive ways by popularizing the mouse as an easy device for controlling the computer (despite its toyish look); introducing the scroll wheel on the original iPod; miniaturizing the storage drive on MP3 players so 1000 songs could be put in your pocket; putting track pads on laptops, eliminating keyboards on phones, and going to a touch-only interface; launching iTunes as the music and video destination for paid content, as well as curating and archiving one's own collections; creating the app store as a global marketplace of iPhone software; making ultrathin and light laptops; catapulting tablets (iPads) to the front lines of customer and business usage; inventing the digital crown for the Apple Watch as a new scrolling mechanism; and much, much more.

Along the way Apple's commitment to employing only the best and most creative solutions made them experts in such areas as chip production, glass technology (Gorilla screens), precision molding (unibody construction); photography (cameras), metallurgy (making their own brand of gold watch casings), battery technology (terraced cells); horology (Apple Watch), health metrics (fitness apps), encryption (iPhones are the toughest to hack in the world), content curation (iTunes), software (MacOS, iOS), marketing (award-winning print and TV ads), customer service (Apple Stores); and more. Apple's impact on the marketplace and culture is unrivaled in history.

HIDDEN TREASURES

Apple's dedication to their craft as shown earlier is extraordinary, but it extends even further. Their sense of care pushes them to perfect even the tiniest details whether people notice it or not. Several examples bear mentioning.

In the early 2000s, Apple incorporated a "breathing status LED indicator" on the front right side of their laptops. The "blinking effect of the sleep mode indicator mimics the rhythm of breathing which is psychologically appealing."[12] That is crazy. What company thinks of (and patents) metering an LED status indicator so it gently flashes on and off in simulation of breathing for psychological comfort? Apple does. When you access Apple Maps' satellite view, you can track the sun's movement across the earth in real time. The white flower petals that open on Apple Watch's time face are not computer-generated photos of blooming flowers but actual blooms that took hundreds of hours to film. Incredibly, Alan Dye, Chief of Human Interface Design at Apple, said the longest shooting took "285 hours and over 24,000 shots."[12] All for a watch face? Similarly, to capture the fluid movements of the jellyfish on another watch face option, Apple built a special tank so they could house and shoot various species of jelly fish swimming in its natural element. And how many people will use the jellyfish watch face? But it doesn't stop there. Jony Ive, Apple's Chief Design Officer, deliberated an entire year on the best method for allowing bands to be swapped out on the Apple Watch, finally settling on a sliding and clicking mechanism that would eliminate the need for any jewelers' tools typically used to change bands. This allowed consumers to customize and change the look of their Apple Watch easily and simply without any visit to the watchmaker.[12] Such creative and intelligent solutions abound at Apple because user experience is central.

Then there is the secret fitness lab Apple built. The lab collected exercise data for two years from employees "running on treadmills, rowing, doing yoga, and wearing masks to measure their breathing changes."[13] This was to create the most accurate fitness app ever by correlating it to real-life, real-time exercise routines. And what about the 800 people working on the iPhone's camera? Apple is not even a camera company and yet it has an army of people dedicated to creating the best smartphone camera possible.[14] Who would have thought it takes 200 parts to make the camera inside Apple's smartphone? Yet all Apple cares about is that the consumer ends up with a great picture. And in the Apple Watch Series 2, Apple made it waterproof by utilizing a very clever piece of engineering; the watch, say after a swim, expels excess droplets out of its tiny speaker ports by using sound vibrations.[15]

All the love and ingenuity invested into Apple's products show why there a sense of glory to them. Though the customer may not be able to explain its magic, it can be felt and experienced. The creative energy put into even the smallest detail shows just how powerful caring deeply can be. It yields crazy, delightful solutions.

In all this, Apple endeared itself to hundreds of millions of people. Apple brought to life the principles of human-centered design way ahead of its time.

EMPATHY OVERPOWERS SPECIFICATIONS

At the core of human-centered design is the idea of empathy, seeing things from the user's perspective rather than from a marketing or selling perspective. Design thinking begins by putting oneself in the shoes of those who will actually use the product or service. As Tim Brown, CEO of IDEO and one of the leaders in the design movement, puts it,

> It's possible to spend days, weeks, or months conducting research, but at the end of it all we will have little more than stacks of field notes, videotapes, and photographs unless we can connect with the people we are observing at a fundamental level. We call this "empathy," and it is perhaps the most important distinction between academic thinking and design thinking. We are not trying to generate new knowledge, test a theory, or validate a scientific hypothesis—that's the work of our university colleagues and an indispensable part of our shared intellectual landscape. The mission of design thinking is to translate observations into insights and insights into products and services that will improve lives.[16]

In other words, design thinking is empathy triumphing over specifications. It rejects any crass ploys to get people to buy something. In design thinking, empathy is the "sacred center" and its purpose is to create "enlightened products." Thus, Apple does not slap together products with off-the-shelf, mass-produced commoditized components. Its products are crafted and brought together with the care of an artisan. Jobs loved to proclaim how they designed products with themselves in mind.

> We made the iPod for ourselves, and when you're doing something for yourself, or your best friend or family, you're not going to cheese out. If you don't love something, you're not going to go the extra mile.[17]

While this might sound selfish, in fact it was high-level design thinking at work. Apple was empathetic to themselves, which was to be empathetic to the user, because they wanted to feel proud of the products that they and their friends and family would use. By making products for themselves, Apple was actually subjecting their design process to the toughest customers they could find and making sure the empathy process would not be short-circuited.

The divide between empathy-based design versus specification-motivated design is stark. IDEO, for example, was asked by Japanese bicycle manufacturer, Shimano, to help it create a breakout product.[18] Shimano seemed to have the technology to stay competitive, but the results weren't showing up. IDEO came along to tackle the problem differently. Instead of considering how to make a bike with more bells and whistles, IDEO did a deep dive into the mind of adult bicyclists. What they found was 90% of adults didn't ride bikes anymore, even though 90% of them had great memories riding bikes as kids. This led to the pivotal insight that adults weren't looking for high-end accessorized bikes; rather, they preferred bikes that could recreate their childhood memories. As a result of this finding, a new category of bikes was created: "coaster bikes" were designed to have the weekender feel with "padded seats, upright handlebars, and puncture-resistant tires [that required] almost no maintenance." Additionally, there were no "controls on the handlebars [or] cables snaking along the frame." It was a total throwback for adults to the charming days when they were young and bikes were easy and carefree to ride. How did IDEO come up with this innovative new category of bikes for Shimano? Through empathy-based insights.

DESIGN THINKING WORKS EVERYWHERE

As design thinkers have opined all along, design thinking's power does not just apply to creating enlightened products; it can also apply to what Horst Rittel (a pioneer in design theory) has termed "wicked problems." By "wicked," Rittel does not mean an "evil" problem; rather, he is referring to problems that are highly resistant and refractory to resolution. Such wicked problems are typically found in the social, political, environmental, or economic space (or in some combined variation of them). They are complicated, interrelated, and very difficult to solve because they can't be controlled like parts on a manufacturing line. Design thinkers say, by using their models with its human-centric approach, great advances and even breakthroughs can be realized. Indeed, both Stanford and IDEO have been applying design thinking to tackle some thorny social issues.

In Hyderabad, India, a villager by the name of Shanti fetches water every day for her family from an open hole in the ground that is about 300 feet from her home. She chooses to get her water from the open source, even though just down the road, only a third of a mile away, a water treatment center offers affordable water that is free of contamination and disease. Why does she choose water from a high-risk source rather than taking a few extra minutes to fetch water from a guaranteed clean source? The issue goes back to how the water treatment system was set up. Visitors that go to the community treatment plant are given five gallons of water per day. Shanti, however, does not have the strength to carry that much water home. The shape of the water container is also problematic in that it precludes Shanti from carrying it on her head or hip. Her husband can't fetch the water because the plant is closed by the time he gets home from work. Additionally, the purchase system is based on a monthly punch card, which forces them to buy more water than they need, thus wasting money. The sum of this system, despite the fact that it provides clean water, is it still does not get the fresh water into the hands of the villagers it was designed to help.

How could this happen? Because the solution providers did not take a hard look at how Shanti and others like her actually go about using and procuring water. They did not properly observe, investigate, or empathize with the end user. Rather than conforming their solution to the villagers, they wanted to conform the villagers to their solution. Without the guiding force of design thinking, the outcome proved to be only minimally helpful.[19]

In contrast, design thinkers, when allowed to tackle a sanitation problem in Kumasi, Ghana, were able to achieve a wonderful outcome. Pay toilets, although dirty and smelly, were relatively well used by local citizens. However, it did not eliminate open defecation in the city. When investigating why this was still happening, it was found that distance to an available toilet played a big role. When people had to get to a toilet quickly but were too far away from the facilities, they would relieve themselves in buckets and then dump its contents into the gutter. Design thinkers realized the solution was not to create more pay toilet sites, but to bring toilet service right to people's homes. This is how "Uniloo" was created; portable toilets were brought to people's homes, with the waste collected two to three times a week. The service was prototyped and proven with 330 initial units, and the rental service model proved so affordable; the project was scaled to 10,000 units.[20]

This success story is representative of the power of design thinking. Observe, research, and empathize with the end user. When you do, the true problem is identified. This allows for effective prototyping to take place. By testing a mini-rollout of a proposed solution, adjustments and corrections can then be made to validate a full-scale implementation. Design process, as predicted, came up with a creative, effective solution to a tough "wicked problem."

The strategic value of design thinking in fields far removed from tech is exciting and heartening, and is showcased here to highlight how Apple's design approach released a tsunami of impact by modeling how to think about solving problems in a human-centered manner. Design thinking can not only propel companies into the future, but interestingly, it also explains how some companies from the past continue to be on today's cutting edge of innovation.

THE BOOKKEEPER WHO CREATED A 100-YEAR-OLD COMPANY: 3M

Minnesota, Mining, and Manufacturing (3M) is known for its innovative ways. It's a company that has been consistently held up as a shining example of how ingenuity and creativity can be integrated into an organization.[21,22] With over $30 billion in revenues, nearly 90,000 employees, and operations in 70 countries,[23] 3M has become one of the giants in corporate America. It is a Fortune Top 100 company, ranked as the 11th best company for leaders, and is included as one of the 30 companies in the Dow Jones Index. It is also one of the companies in the S&P 500.[24] Most impressive is that the company sells over 55,000 products, churns out 20 new products every week,[25,26] and has been awarded over 105,000 patents.[23] These last two numbers speak volumes to the innovative spirit at the company.

Founded in 1902 with the purpose of finding minerals in northern Minnesota, how did 3M come to be this engine of innovation? How did it create such a diversity of products? The company counts itself as having 46 technology platforms—from adhesives to microreplication to light management—with over 8300 researchers worldwide; 4500 in the United States alone.[23] How did 3M come to create such a unique culture of inventors and innovators?

The key architect of 3M's innovative culture was a young man by the name of William McKnight. Originally hired as a bookkeeper in 1906, he quickly began making his mark in the company by working directly with customers to solve problems. That simple but pivotal habit turned into what can now be called a prequel to the design movement. From those interactions, McKnight would leverage insights from his customers into products, and later as he was promoted into management, he would scale what he learned into a culture of innovation for the entire company. He became president in 1929 and chairman of the board in 1949.

His idea of working directly with customers (as opposed to conceiving things in the laboratory) would later be given the fancy academic term, "lead user process," which states innovation results best from working with the primary user.[27] This practice of interfacing with the "lead user" was actually a foreshadow of empathy-based thinking. By getting on the ground and working with the intended user from the start, McKnight was utilizing design principles that would not be codified until nearly 100 years later.

Essential to McKnight's thinking was the thought that failure did not have to be fatal. McKnight stated,

> Mistakes will be made, but if the man is essentially right himself, I think the mistakes he makes are not so serious in the long run as the mistakes management makes if it is dictatorial and if it undertakes to tell men... exactly how they must do their job. Management that is destructively critical when mistakes are made kills initiative. And it's essential that we have many people with initiative if we are to continue to grow.[28]

In essence, McKnight was setting a culture of creative activity and prototyping by making sure management did not squelch initiative. Successive iteration is one of the key practices of the creative process. Jony Ive was known to make hundreds of prototypes before settling on a final version. McKnight thus helped create an environment in which employees could experiment without fear and leverage insights from failures into steps toward ultimate success. These seminal ideas became known as the McKnight Principles, with McKnight elaborating on them in pithy, practical ways. The revered leader of 59 years stated, "Encourage experimental doodling. If you put fences around people, you get sheep. Give people the room they need."[29] And then this simple maxim: "Listen to anybody with an idea."[30]

McKnight wanted people's minds to roam, to think associatively, and to be free to think outside the box as they pondered how to solve problems. This is also a key to design strategy. As stated by Tom and David Kelly, founders of IDEO and the famed d.school at Stanford University, "Creativity comes into play wherever you have the opportunity to generate new ideas, solutions, or approaches. We think of creativity as using your imagination to create something new in the world."[31]

McKnight's insight into the creative impulses of workers was way ahead of its time. Long before "innovate or die" became the mantra of the day, McKnight had already acted to instill it in the company's culture.[28] In 1948, "after the development of masking tape, McKnight learned a crucial lesson about letting his engineers follow their instincts. He soon codified this lesson into a policy known as the 15% rule, which lets 3M engineers spend up to 15% of their work time pursuing whatever project they like."[30] This rule would serve to unleash enormous innovation in the company. The most famous brainchild of the 15% rule was Art Fry's invention of the *Post-It Notes*, which has become one of the best-selling office products of all time.[32,33] Says Kurt Beinlich of the 15% rule, a technical director for 3M, "It's really shaped what and who 3M is."[32]

The effect of McKnight's leadership philosophy was to set a powerful course for 3M. Richard Carlton, 3M's director of manufacturing and author of its first testing manual, wrote, "Every idea should have a chance to prove its worth, and this is true for two reasons: (1) If it is good, we want it; (2) if it is not good, we will have purchased peace of mind when we have proved it impractical." And Carlton would add, "You can't stumble if you're not in motion."[30]

BUILT FOR BRILLIANCE

In addition to unleashing its employees with the 15% rule, 3M also moved to vertically integrate a similar rule at the organizational level. In 1993, they implemented the 30% rule, which required each of the company's operating divisions to derive 30% of its revenues from new products introduced in the previous 4 years.[29] Formally referred to as the "New Product Vitality Index (NPVI)," it represented 3M's ongoing commitment to stay on the cutting edge. While the company continued to enjoy robust sales from its historical inventions like *Scotch tape*, 3M has never lost its drive to bring new products to market. "In 2008, 3M calculated its NPVI at 25%. In 2012, its NPVI was 33%. The company is shooting for an NPVI of 40% by 2017."[34]

That the company was set up to constantly invite and honor creativity bears witness to Geoff Colvin's idea, senior editor at Fortune magazine, that some companies are "built for brilliance."[35] Indeed, the fruit that has dropped from 3M's tree has delighted many around the world. Some major milestones are as follows[28]:

- 1920: The first waterproof sandpaper invented; reduces airborne dust (construction and automotive industry).
- 1925: Scotch tape is born (office).
- 1940: Reflective sheeting for highway markings (safety).
- 1950: Scotchgard Fabric Protector (furniture and clothes); Scotch-Brite Cleaning Pads (kitchen).
- 1955: Metered-dose inhaler ("puffers" for asthmatics; medical).
- 1960: Overhead projectors, carbonless paper (office).
- 1967: Littman stethoscopes (doctors).
- 1979: Thinsulate (winter coats; roof fabric coating in Porsche and Jaguar convertibles).
- 1980: Post-it Notes (office).
- 1990: Flexible circuits (electronics).
- 2004: Transparent duct tape (consumer).
- 2007: ScotchBlue Painter's Tape for Corners and Hinges (construction).

- 2009: Bluetooth-enabled Littman stethoscope; wirelessly transfers heart /lung data.
- 2012: Solar mirror for concentrating solar power (energy).

This is a track record that few companies in the world can match (and it represents only a small sampling of 3M's industry-leading products). 3M has stayed in the game for a long time and is still a leader after an incredible 114 years. This is a testament to the power of putting creativity at the center of a company's culture. While it's said that "innovation and creativity are now widely accepted as the driving forces behind business success, and are among the most highly prized qualities in today's leaders,"[36] McKnight proved he was a leader way ahead of his time. He became a Minnesota miracle. By setting up 3M to be a place of ingenuity and creativity, he was creating a titanium-strength culture that has thrived for over a century.[35] Creativity is an expression of caring. And when you care, the end result can be crazy and delightful. From Post-it Notes to iPhones, 3M and Apple have shown the fun and power of innovation.

BOOT CAMP #6: NEW THINKING

1. When was the last time you engaged in new thinking and implemented it?

2. How did it turn out?

3. How do you stimulate new thinking in your life?

Section III

Disruption: Global Arena

Progression to Impact

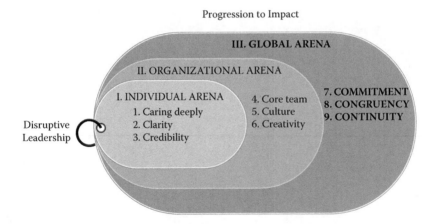

FIGURE S.III
Key chain.

8

Commitment: Caring Executes and Overcomes All Obstacles

It's not done until it ships.[1]

—**Steve Jobs**

This short phrase represents one of the great secrets of Apple's enormous disruptive powers. While Apple is often celebrated as the most creative company in the world,[2,3] its culture of execution is not given enough credit. Behind the enormous imagination of the company is an equally enormous ability to execute on that imagination. Jobs' philosophy of "shipping" set up an organizational imperative that put execution at the forefront of everyone's minds.

In many ways, the domain of disruption is reducible to this singular ability to execute. All the ideas in the world, all the heart-warming aspirations are for naught if there is no follow-through. Once a dream is born in a leader, that is just the beginning. The process of realizing a vision is the hard part; it's the perspiration side of inspiration.

Legendary leader Jack Welsh, former Chairman and CEO of General Electric, has put it in the most vivid of terms, "In real life, strategy is actually very straight forward. You pick a general direction and implement like hell."[4]

For Jobs and company, there was no dichotomy between idea and completion. It was just one long thought. Caring forces completion. It gets the job done and it weathers all kinds of difficulties to get there. For leaders that are disruptive, their sense of responsibility and mission precludes any thought of dropping the ball. As Larry Bossidy, former CEO of Honeywell, has said, "Every great leader has an instinct for execution. He [says], 'Unless I can make this plan happen, it's not going to matter.'"[5]

As stated in his best-selling book, *Execution*, Bossidy defines execution as[6]

1. The missing link
2. The main reason companies fall short in their promises
3. The gap between what a company's leaders want to achieve and the ability of their organizations to deliver it
4. Not simply tactics but a system of getting things done through questioning, analysis, and follow-through
5. A central part of a company's strategy and its goals and the major job of any leader in business
6. A discipline requiring a comprehensive understanding of a business, its people, and its environment
7. The way to link the three core processes of any business—the people process, the strategy, and the operating plan—together to get things done on time

By these criteria, it can be seen why Apple is such a powerhouse. They don't lack the missing link of execution. They do not fall short in their promises. There is no gap between what the company wants to achieve and what it delivers. Execution is not a tactic; it's part of their identity. And they are fierce warriors in the discipline of getting things done. They are the best of the best, or as Kahney has stated, "Apple has been distinguished by superb execution on all fronts: products, sales, marketing, and support."[7] How has Apple accomplished this? Four pillars can be noted.

EXECUTING THROUGH CRYSTAL CLEAR GOALS

One of Jobs' great leadership skills was to clear the clutter and articulate what the company had to be about. As previously noted, simplicity was a religion at Apple.

Simplicity, however, was not only the goal of Apple products; it also applied to how the company was run and the strategy behind its goals. During Jobs' years of exile (1985–1997), the company had lost its "simple" ways and created "a bewildering [array] of computer models, including Quadra, Performa, Macintosh LC, PowerBook, and Power Macintosh. The sheer number of choices was creating confusion for Apple's customers and employees alike. It was bad business all the way around."[8]

When Jobs returned to lead Apple, one of his first acts was to blow up the confusing product mix by implementing a radical simplification of what Apple was going to do:

> [It was] a square containing four quadrants. What it represented was Apple's new product strategy. He was going to transition Apple from its multitude of computer models to a simple grid of four: laptops for consumers and pros and desktops for consumers and pros. It was one of the most dramatic minimizations of a product line in technology history. Steve's simple graphic was both an example of Simplicity and a corporate road map. This chart made it clear to every Apple employee where the company was going. With one simple image, Steve moved Apple from a truckload of models to a handful. He set the company off on a wild spree of invention, providing inspiration for the engineers and expectations for the customers.[8]

Jobs was able to lead Apple into incredible feats of execution because their energies were not dispersed all over the place. Instead, their goals were clear and focused. Not only would their products be beautiful; their product strategy would be as well. Executing to that "box" would be the new mandate.

EXECUTING THROUGH AGGRESSIVE DEADLINES

Deadlines are a time-tested and traditional tool for driving execution. However, from his front row seat, Segall observed some nuances on how Apple was able to achieve world-class performance:

> Project timelines come in several varieties. They can be leisurely, compressed, relaxed, or impossible. Though it may defy logic, the easiest way

to screw up a project is to give it too much time—enough time for people to rethink, revise, have second thoughts, invite others into the project, get more opinions, conduct tests, etc. Leonard Bernstein captured this thought perfectly when he said: "To achieve great things, two things are needed; a plan, and not quite enough time."[9]

The key phrase here is "not quite enough time." Jobs would first provide the big-picture goals and directions of where Apple was headed and then drive execution with project deadlines that would stretch people's capacity, even to the point they weren't sure they could achieve it. Jobs would set deadlines that seemed impossible, but they weren't unreachable; they just required an extra level of determination and grit. Jobs was able to draw out the highest potential and talent in people by using deadlines in the most strategic of manners—don't give them too much time or just enough time, rather, not quite enough time. The idea was to keep the company in motion, always moving ahead and innovating. Citing Bob Dylan (recent Nobel Prize Winner in Literature) and The Beatles as artists who kept "evolving, moving, refining their art," Jobs shared, "that's what I've always tried to do—keep moving. Otherwise as Dylan says, if you're not busy being born, you're busy dying."[10] For Jobs, the use of aggressive timelines exhibited his "bias for action," which management guru Tom Peters States is the number one attribute of companies that excel.

EXECUTING THROUGH ACCOUNTABILITY

One of the things less noted about Jobs was his monster work ethic. Leading a disruptive company required deep dedication and sacrifice. Jobs worked long hours each week because he was involved in directing so many areas. Most management theories espouse efficiency through delegation but Jobs batted away that notion by being intimately involved in multiple areas, from product design to advertisement. While this in part represented Jobs' penchant for control, it also represented another reason why Apple was so good at execution. Jobs made himself the person accountable for the work being done in most strategic areas of the company. He kept things on schedule, and he was the quality control person. He made sure the Apple brand kept humming along at only the highest levels. His attention to Apple's marketing efforts provides a key example. Segall writes,

> He knew that if he participated in the marketing process, directing a small group of smart people, Apple would continue to market circles around its competitors. Steve didn't believe in delegating significant marketing decisions to others. He was there for every presentation and stayed current with every project's progress. During the "Think Different" years, I can personally attest that he was involved with every image and every word. Not tyrannically so, but as an eager participant. I lost track of the number of midnight phone calls we had just to go over the copy for an ad about to be published. Steve enforced one policy I've never seen implemented anywhere else. I wouldn't be surprised if he was the only big-company CEO on earth who worked this way. He wouldn't allow anyone to see the agency's creative ideas before he did. He didn't want anyone, even the VP of marketing, to filter the work before he had a chance to view it. "I don't want someone guessing what I'm going to like or not like," Steve explained on more than one occasion. "Maybe I'll see a spark in there that nobody else sees."[11]

This idea of accountability was not just something Jobs assigned to himself. He built it into the company to create maximal effectiveness and execution. He strove to strip any ambiguity as to where the buck stopped and who was responsible for a project's success or demise. Jobs abhorred the idea of committees, stating, "The reason you have committees is that you have divided responsibilities. We don't. At Apple you can figure out exactly who is responsible."[12] As a result, the concept of DRI (Directly Responsible Individual) was created to represent "the person on any given assignment who [would] be called on the carpet if something [wasn't] done right."

> Jobs insisted on a clear chain of command all the way down the line: everyone in the company knew whom they reported to and what was expected of them. "The organization is clean and simple to understand, and very accountable," Jobs told Business Week.[7]

> Reported one departed employee, "There's no confusion as to who's going to do what. It's very detail-oriented. I tried to bring this to other places, and they were like, 'What do you mean?' They wanted two to three people to

have responsibility." The DRI is a powerful management tool, enshrined as an Apple corporate best practice.[13]

The DRI concept is an Apple best practice for good reason. It's a system of transparency for accomplishment and glory (or for embarrassment). Either way, it's imbued the company with a sense of being on its toes, staying active, and making sure Apple shipped the products the public was waiting for.

EXECUTING THROUGH A STRONG WILL

Jobs' passion for making world-changing products gave him a continuous sense of urgency and the heart of an overcomer; he wouldn't allow things to deter him from that mission. As a result, much of what was accomplished at Apple was a function of his zeal and strong will. This meant, in many cases, he would not take "no" for an answer. If they had committed to a deadline, then they had committed, and it would get done at all costs. The launch of the Macintosh computer was a great case in point.

On the heels of Apple II and Apple III, Jobs was itching to launch the company's next big thing. The Macintosh had all the signs of being the company's next blockbuster product, and with the Microsoft–IBM alliance on the rise, Jobs knew that timing for the Macintosh's release was crucial. The Macintosh had to get into the hands of consumers soon in order to head off the PC juggernaut.

Whipping up enthusiasm and expectations—as Jobs was so good at doing—Monday, January 16, 1984 was the slated date for shipping units to dealers. However, the software side had not been completed. Led by Andy Hertzfield, the coding team told Jobs despite their valiant efforts they would need one extra week. The computers could be released with a "demo" status and updated with the final version one week later. Jobs would have nothing of it. "There's no way we're slipping!" he bellowed. The software team was crestfallen. They needed just one more week after months of intense coding, and it made sense that they could buy one extra week with a "demo" designation. But Jobs was dead set against it and demanded all hands on deck to see the deadline met. Sure enough, fueled by "chocolate-covered espresso beans," the team pulled three consecutive all-nighters and delivered on time. Once again, "Jobs' reality distortion field pushed them to do what they had thought impossible."[14]

The payoff? When Jobs introduced the Mac at the Flint Center in Cupertino to an overflowing, buzzing crowd of 2600 people, the audience began to surge with excitement at what they were witnessing—scrolling text, talking introductions, and moving graphics. They started to cheer and clap. By the end of the presentation, everyone was on their feet:

> Pandemonium erupted, with people in the crowd jumping up and down and pumping their fists in a frenzy. Jobs nodded slowly, a tight-lipped but broad smile on his face, then looked down and started to choke up. The ovation continued for five minutes.[15]

Despite the excruciating pain it took to deliver the Mac on time, it was now on full display before the whole world. Rather than limping in as a demo unit, a new category of DOA was created—disruptive on arrival. No product introduction had ever been met with a five-minute standing ovation. Without Jobs' sense of mission and strong-willed leadership, the team would not have achieved history. Executing never felt better.

All this serves to underscore Bossidy's maxim that "Execution is a leader's most important job." When a leader gets that right, he or she gets a lot right. Just ask the coffee industry after Howard Schultz appeared on the scene. He turned the traditional, slow-as-molasses coffee world upside down.

ITALY IN A CUP: STARBUCKS

Starbucks is the largest coffee chain in the world. Started in 1971 as a solo coffee shop in Seattle's historic Pike Place Market, it has gone on to become the undisputed global leader, recognizable to any coffee lover in the world. So dominant is it in the U.S. market that it accounts for over 70% of the total U.S. coffee and snack industry's revenues ($29 Bln).[16] No other coffee chain is even close, domestically or internationally.

With annual revenues of over $21 billion, it is miles ahead of its next global competitors, Tim Hortons ($3.2 billion), Panera Bread ($2.5 billion), and Costa Coffee ($1.5 billion). In terms of storefronts, Starbucks has more than 23,000 stores worldwide, dramatically outdistancing its closest rivals, McCafe (5,044 stores) and Costa Coffee (3,036 stores).[17] After going public in 1992, its current market value is at $78 billion—an unbelievable leap from its humble beginnings.

Coffee is the second most traded commodity in the world, worth over $100 billion. Only crude oil tops it. So beloved is coffee that natural gas, gold, wheat, and cotton rank below it.[18,19] Worldwide, over 500 billion cups of coffee are drunk every year. The average American drinks three and half cups each day. Not surprisingly, 75% of Americans' caffeine source comes from coffee.[18]

Yet despite its ubiquity, the habit of drinking coffee had barely changed over the previous 100 years, that is, until Starbucks came along. How did Starbucks break out like a comet in an industry that people proclaimed could never be a growth industry? Data showed coffee consumption had been in decline since the mid-1960s while soft drinks took over as the country's favorite drink.[20] How did Schultz "reinvent an age-old commodity" that was content with its main street, thermos-filling persona? He did it by associating it with a new kind of experience. He did it by putting Italy in a cup.

Originally captivated by Starbucks' missionary-like zeal in providing the best roasted coffee beans (but not the drink itself), Schultz was catapulted to another realm of coffee ecstasy when he was sent to Milan on company business. Within days of being immersed in Italian culture, he was mesmerized by the "ritual and romance of coffee bars in Italy."[21] Espresso bars were everywhere. Baristas made their espressos with flair, skill, and personality. It was fun to watch. Engaging. It wasn't just a neat experience; it was "great theater."[22] While reveling in this new found world, thunder struck for Schultz:

> Serving espresso drinks the Italian way could be *the differentiating factor* for Starbucks. If we could re-create in America the authentic Italian coffee bar culture, it might resonate with other Americans the way it did with me. Starbucks could be a great experience, and not just a great retail store.

I watched as the barista made a shot of espresso, steamed a frothy pitcher of milk, and poured the two into a cup, with a dollop of foam on the top. Here was the perfect balance between steamed milk and coffee, combining espresso, which is the noble essence of coffee, and milk made sweet by steaming rather than by adding sugar. It was the perfect drink. Of all the coffee experts I had met, none had ever mentioned this drink. *No one in America knows about this, I thought. I've got to take it back with me.*[23]

DELIVERING ITALY IN A CUP IS NO CUP OF TEA

And so it was in the charming sidewalk cafes of Milan that Schultz's heart was stolen. He had to bring that romantic feeling of coffee with its atmosphere of community and fraternity back to America. He possessed a new found conviction that this was the way to share great coffee with friends and help make the world a little better. Filled with excitement, he returned to Seattle with anticipation. But his dream would be met with hesitancy, resistance, and obstacles. Schultz would have to overcome many mountains, which is why he later confessed, Starbucks' success "is as much one of perseverance and drive as it is of talent and luck."[24]

Partner Obstacles

Schultz thought he had a way to turbocharge the business. The Italy in a cup concept was a game changer. But when presented to his bosses, the idea fell on deaf ears. Schultz described the experience this way:

> Have you ever had a brilliant idea—one that blows you away—only to have the people who can make it a reality tell you it's not worth pursuing? That's what happened to me on my return to Seattle from Italy. I thought I'd come upon a truly extraordinary insight, one that could serve as the foundation for a whole new industry and change the way Americans drank coffee. To my bosses, however, I was an overexcited marketing director. Starbucks was a retailer—not a restaurant or a bar, they argued. Serving espresso drinks would put them in the beverage business, a move they feared would dilute the integrity of what they envisioned the mission of a coffee store to be.[25]

Disappointed but undeterred, Schultz continued to work his angle and after a year of nagging, it was agreed Schultz could test his espresso bar idea. As Starbucks opened up its sixth store in the heart of Seattle's business district, they gave him a tiny space of 300 square feet to set up shop. It was in April 1984. Schultz was giddy with excitement. This would be the moment when he would show his partners that the romance of Italy in a cup made by espresso-obsessed baristas would capture the imagination of coffee drinkers everywhere. When the doors opened at 7 am, traffic started slow but began to crescendo as the day wore on. Customers came in and quizzically ordered "cafe latte." They could barely pronounce the name but the baristas were there to caringly and enthusiastically educate them on this new kind of drink. As customers took their first sips, they became part of history without knowing it. Schultz said, "As far as I know, America was first introduced to caffe latte that morning," and by the end of the day, "Starbucks had entered a different business."[26] Its opening day was a big success. Instead of serving the projected 250 customers, 400 brave individuals had queued up to give "espresso" a go. In the couple months to follow, traffic continued growing, reaching 800 customers served a day.[27] Schultz couldn't have been happier with the overwhelming response and all the while using just 300 square feet of retail space.[27] Surely, this would be the proof that Starbucks needed to grow beyond its roasted bean strategy. The future was serving the actual drink.

Incredibly, Schultz's partners did not agree. The great chasm in opinion came down to what Starbucks would stand for, what its identity would be. As Jerry Baldwin, president at that time, would say, "We're coffee roasters. I don't want to be in the restaurant business. I'm sorry, Howard. We aren't going to do it. You'll have to live with that."[28] After a year and half of struggle, it had come down to this. The fault lines had crystallized. Schultz would have no opportunity to grow his idea inside of Starbucks:

> I was depressed for months, paralyzed by uncertainty. I felt torn in two by conflicting feelings: loyalty to Starbucks and confidence in my vision for Italian-style espresso bars. I was busy enough with my everyday work that I could have distracted myself and just dropped the idea. But I refused to let it die. The espresso business felt too right, and my instincts about it ran too deep to let it go.[29]

His partners proved to be greater obstacles than he ever anticipated. He wanted to bring about "sea change for the company,"[30] but they didn't see it that way. It was time to strike out on his own. Reluctantly, Schultz left Starbucks.

Money Obstacles

By 1985, Schultz had formed his own venture and named it Il Giornale (Italian for "daily"). Ironically, Gordon Bowker, one of Starbucks' resistant partners, but who agreed to serve as consultant to Schultz for 6 months, came up with the name. Doubly ironic, Jerry Baldwin, Starbucks' president, offered to invest $150,000 in Il Giornale.[31] Despite the fact that both partners didn't want to be in the espresso business, they still volunteered to help the start-up. Schultz was grateful for the vote of confidence and comforted to know there were no hard feelings.

The $150,000 was a sizable investment, but Schultz calculated he needed $1.7 million of seed money to launch up to eight espresso bars.[32] The initial strategy was to go to Italy and excite investors there with how their way of making coffee would revolutionize coffee drinking in America. Surely, Schultz could land a million dollar investment with an Italian group that loved the idea of spreading espresso to their American compatriots. The idea, however, found no welcoming parties; "Americans, they insisted, could never enjoy espresso the way Italians do."[33] Schultz had visited a dizzying 500 espresso places, but the well turned up dry. Despite returning with no money, Schultz was still pumped about getting Il Giornale off the ground.

Upon returning to the States, Schultz resorted to a new ground game. If raising the capital couldn't be accomplished by impressing a few big investors, he would take his plans and pitch it one-by-one to others. Over the course of the next year, Schultz would share his idea with 242 people; 217 of them said "no." That translated to nearly a 90% rejection rate. Yet through sheer willpower and determination, Schultz did it. He raised his $1.7 million spread across 25 investors. Il Giornale was born. In April 1986, exactly two years after Schultz's first espresso bar concept, the first store was opened, a charming 700-square-foot site near Seattle's tallest building. In time, over 1000 customers were being served each day. Schultz's dream was off and running.

Traitors in the Camp

Serendipitously, less than a year later, in March 1987, Schultz' original partners, Jerry Baldwin and Gordon Bowker, decided to sell Starbucks, which included six stores, a roasting plant, and most importantly, its name and brand.[34] For Schultz, it was a no-brainer. He had to buy the company where it all began for him. But the price was daunting. Raising $1.7 million to finance II Giornale was a feat; buying Starbucks would cost $4 million. Nevertheless, it seemed like destiny for Schultz to purchase Starbucks, until it wasn't.

Inexplicably, or motivated by pride and greed, one of Schultz's II Giornale investors decided to submit a competing bid. It was an uncoordinated bid, clearly designed to get an upper hand over Schultz and reduce his role in the company. Schultz was shocked by the move and decided the only way to confront the matter was to have a face-to-face meeting. Soliciting Bill Gates Sr.'s support (father of Microsoft founder Bill Gates), Schultz arranged a meeting with the senior Gates at his side:

> The day of our meeting was one of the toughest, most painful of my life. I had no idea how it would turn out, and my life's work was at stake. As I walked in, my opponent sat at the head of a conference table, larger than life, in full command of the room. Without even waiting to hear me out, he began blasting me. "We've given you the chance of a lifetime. We invested in you when you were nothing. You're still nothing. Now you have an opportunity to buy Starbucks. But it's our money. It's our idea. It's our business. This is how we're going to do it, with or without you." He sat back before delivering the ultimatum: "If you don't take this deal, you'll never work again in this town. You'll never raise another dollar. You'll be dog meat."[35]

The attack was brazen. It was traitorous. They had fronted some of the money to start II Giornale, and now they felt they could control the business. It was a moment of crisis. Schultz recounted,

> When the meeting ended, I walked out and started to cry, right there in the lobby. Bill Gates tried to reassure me that everything would turn out all right, but he was aghast about the outburst at the meeting. That night, when I got home, I felt as though my life had ended. "There's no hope," I told Sheri [Schultz's wife] "I don't know how I'm going to raise the money. I don't know

what we're going to do." This was a turning point in my life. If I had agreed to the terms that investor demanded, he would have taken my dream from me. He could have fired me at whim and dictated the atmosphere and values of Starbucks. The passion, the commitment, and the dedication that made it thrive would have all disappeared.[36]

But Schultz steeled himself. He was committed to crushing the challenge:

> Many of us face critical moments in our lives, when our dreams seem ready to shatter. You can never prepare for such events, but how you react to them is crucial. It is important to remember your values: Be bold, but be fair. Don't give in. It's the time your strength is tested most tellingly.[37]

Schultz would not fold. Garnering the support of his other II Giornale investors, Schultz built a coalition with his remaining supporters, and in a matter of weeks came up with $3.8 million to purchase Starbucks.[36] Five months later in August of 1987, the deal was sealed. II Giornale was folded into the original Starbucks as it was always meant to be. Schultz had won another war, and Starbucks was reborn.

CREATING NEW PARADIGMS IN COFFEE: SECOND WAVE AND THIRD PLACE

Through all of Schultz's struggles, his vision for Starbucks never wavered. His passion for enhancing people's lives through a romantic notion of Italian-made espresso was heartfelt. It was deep. It was a way to touch people's lives by giving them a bit of joy in a cup. In the process, Starbucks unleashed the Second Wave of Coffee.

The First Wave of Coffee could be traced back to the 1800s when brands like Folgers (*"The Best Part of Waking Up"*), Maxwell House (*"Good to The Last Drop"*), Hills Bros. (who invented vacuum packaging to keep beans fresher for longer), and Nescafe (instant coffee) made their way en masse into American kitchens and people's daily routines.[38] But when Starbucks introduced the espresso to America, it elevated coffee drinking to another level and the public fell in love with the beauty of specialty-made coffees. It became a new wave, a second wave of coffee experience never previously imagined.

Starbucks single-handedly pioneered and popularized it. Who would have thought people would pay three to four dollars for a cup of coffee when they were used to twenty-five cent cups at the local diner? Yet the value proposition was so powerful, millions made Starbucks their morning ritual.

Additionally, Starbucks pioneered the idea of going to a dedicated brick and mortar place for coffee (as opposed to truck stops, convenient stores, or restaurants) and thereby framed for coffee lovers an added experience never previously thought of. Coffee could be used to create a psychological anchor for taking breaks or gearing up for the day. Starbucks stores have thus become known as the "The Third Place," i.e., "a comfortable, sociable gathering spot away from home and work."[39] Schultz attributes this Third Place phenomenon to (1) a taste of romance, (2) an affordable luxury, (3) an oasis, and (4) casual social interactions.[40] All these speak, as has been mentioned, to the disruptive impact human-centric designs can have.

Schultz's mention of "oasis" points to something deeply insightful. There is a need to take mental breaks and have "mini down-times" so folks can step away for a few moments to clear their heads before "getting back at it." This speaks to our rhythm of work, i.e., spurts of activity need to be punctuated by moments of respite. The idea of being a "casual gathering place" understates the charm of Starbucks stores. Starbucks stores are designed and architected to hug people with warmth and comfort. Given a choice, people will always prefer this to a pigeon-stained park bench or plastic tables at McDonald's. By combining a great cup of coffee with a sense of place, Starbucks devised a compelling new experience that won over the world. They've succeeded wildly in connecting with the coffee lover. All this on the account of one man's desire to "help make the world a little better" and his unwillingness to stop short of achieving that.

When you're committed, you will always find a way. Obstacles will assert themselves. Difficulties will abound. But the leader that cares deeply overcomes. Jobs did it. Schultz did it. Apple and Starbucks would not be the leaders they are today without Jobs and Schultz's deep commitment to the discipline of executing.

**BOOT CAMP #7: EXECUTION
AND FOLLOW-THROUGH**

1. Share an "overcoming story" you've been through in pursuit of your own *personal* goals. Why were you motivated to push through? Do you think this kind of experience can translate into how you lead your company? If so, has it happened and what was it?

2. Share a "regret" story of when you failed to deliver. What did you learn from it?

3. Besides Jobs and Schultz's, recount another example of perseverance and determination that has inspired you. How can you apply this to your leadership?

9

Congruency: Staying Fiercely True to the Call of Caring

We believe that we are on the face of the earth to make great products and that's not changing[1]

—Tim Cook, CEO, Apple

With success come distractions. As expertise and reputation of a company grow, a multitude of new directions and initiatives can be had. Everyone wants a piece of you. Everyone is suggesting what you can or should do next. Apple should buy Yahoo. Apple should buy Netflix. Apple should buy Uber. The chorus is endless. But disruptive leaders know how to stick to their calling. They don't deviate from their values or mission. And at Apple, anything which is incongruent to the mission of making great products is weeded out and eliminated. Alignment is king.

THE ART OF REFUSAL

Steve Jobs had a wonderful insight into how congruency and disruption were connected when he stated, "Focus is not saying yes. It is saying no to really great ideas."[2] This principle became central to Apple's decision making process. "The ability to say no—to reject features, products, categories, market segments, deals, and even certain partners—is how Steve Jobs explained Apple's core strengths. 'Focusing is powerful,' he said."[3] "His management mantra was focus."[4]

The discipline to stay on task has been crucial to Apple's success. Jobs taught, "Strategy is figuring out what not to do,"[5] and he loved the notion of "less is more" and "elegance is refusal."[2] The power of restraint was something Jobs mastered deeply. A former executive stated,

> Apple is not set up to do twenty amazing things a year. At most it's three projects that can get a ton of attention at the executive level. It is about editing down. The executive team is always looking at picking technologies at just the right time. The minute you're doing a hundred things, you can't possibly do things the Apple way. Most companies don't want to focus on one thing because they could fail. Winnowing ideas from twenty-five to four is horrifyingly scary.[6]

While cutting down to a few projects might be horrifying for many CEOs, for Jobs it was exhilarating. "We look at a lot of things, but I'm as proud of the products that we have not done as I am of the ones we have done."[7] As current CEO Tim Cook likes to point out, "Apple [can] put its entire product line on a conference room table."[8] As a result, a lot has been left on Apple's cutting room floor—personal digital assistants, monitors, laser printers, clones, to name a few; these were all distractions Jobs felt Apple couldn't afford.[9] Although each of these products could have been strong money makers in their own right, they were incongruent with Apple's commitment to "less is more." In this regard, Apple's propensity to say no to such profit opportunities is an outrageous act of "revenue avoidance."[6] Yet Apple has lost no sleep over this approach.

> PC makers put crapware on their computers—antivirus software, subscription offers, and so on—precisely because the revenue is lucrative. Apple forgoes such opportunities time and again, convinced that high-quality products will ultimately generate more profits.[10]

To underscore Jobs' "disregard" for money, Apple has intentionally ignored the business market or enterprise segment in order to focus on bringing its products to the people. To many, this was leaving millions if not billions of dollars of revenue on the table:

> There have been calls for Apple to sell to big business. Jobs has resisted because selling to companies—no matter how big the potential market—is outside of Apple's focus. "The roots of Apple were to build computers for people, not for corporations," Jobs has said. "The world doesn't need another Dell or Compaq."[7]

How many leaders have the fortitude to say no to this kind of opportunity? Then again, how many understand the power of staying true to their core values no matter how tempting the situation may be?

CONGRUENCY MEETS BLUE OCEAN

In 2005, Professors W. Chan Kim and Renee Mauborgne at INSEAD published their seminal book *Blue Ocean Strategy*. Backed by extensive research gathered across 30 industries and spanning 100 years of business practice, the authors provided a framework for helping companies expand into uncontested markets instead of competing in existing ones (blue versus red oceans). A critical component of their strategy is helping leaders focus in the right place through their Blue Ocean Leadership Grid, which is defined as "an analytical tool that challenges people to think about which acts and activities leaders should *do less of* because they hold people back, and which leaders should *do more of* because they inspire people to give it their all."[11] The leadership grid is actually a simple four-question test.[11]

On the "do less" side are two questions:

1. ELIMINATE. "What acts and activities do leaders invest their time and intelligence in that should be eliminated?"
2. REDUCE. "What acts and activities do leaders invest their time and intelligence in that should be reduced well below their current levels?"

On the "do more" side are two questions as well:

3. RAISE. "What acts and activities do leaders invest their time and intelligence in that should be raised well above their current levels?"
4. CREATE. "What acts and activities should leaders invest their time and intelligence in that they currently don't undertake?"

The sum total of responses to these four questions is to increase the efficiency and focus of leaders so their strategic decisions move the company to uncreated and uncontested markets where they can establish themselves as champions in that segment. This is how businesses "win the future," which reiterates Alan Kay's widely quoted maxim, "The best way to predict the future is to invent it."[12]

When viewed through this grid, it can be seen why Jobs and Apple have continually harvested blue ocean opportunities. They have always invented their way into spaces never previously imagined (although in a hybrid fashion as opposed to pure blue ocean theory since Apple blasted open new vistas in contested segments). And how did they do this? By following the principle of congruence, which was to continually ask "are we doing the right things?" Should we eliminate or reduce our focus in certain areas, or should we raise our focus or establish new ones? The answers to these questions create important downstream implications as it will either "hold people back" or "inspire people to give it their all."[11] Once again, we see how modern business theories have come along to substantiate many of Jobs' intuitive practices that served as key components for Apple's success. Learning to stay focused and congruent was one of them. Interestingly, one of Jobs' keen interests was not in an area most business schools would teach CEOs to focus on. Yet for Jobs, it was an essential activity.

JOBS' LOVE OF MARKETING

Jobs was crazy about marketing. Why did he insist on knowing all the minutiae of the next campaign? Segall has written that for Jobs, "Marketing is the context for just about everything. It's not an exaggeration to say that marketing is as critical to Apple's success as the devices the company makes."[13] Could this be true, or is it an overstatement? Could marketing at Apple actually be on par with making great products? To understand this proposition, one has to understand how Jobs viewed marketing. Marketing did not exist to sell. Marketing existed to communicate the company's heart beat. In Jobs' words,

> To me, *marketing is about values.* This is a very complicated world, it's a very noisy world, and we're not going to get a chance to get people to remember much about us. No company is. And so we have to be really clear on what we want them to know about us. The way to do that is not to talk about speeds and feeds. It's not to talk about MIPS and megahertz. It's not to talk about why we're better than Windows.

The dairy industry tried for twenty years to convince you that milk was good for you. And the sales have gone like this [down], and then they tried "Got milk?" and the sales have gone like this [up]. "Got Milk?" doesn't even talk about the price—matter of fact the focus is on the absence of the price.

[So]...our customers want to know, "Who is Apple, and what is it that we stand for? Where do we sit in this world?" And what we're about isn't making boxes for people to get their jobs done, although we do that well. We do that better than almost anybody in some cases. But Apple is about something more than that. Apple at the core, is that we believe that people with passion can change the world for the better. That's what we believe. . . . And that those people who are crazy enough to think they can change the world are the ones that actually do.[14]

There it was. Jobs' love of marketing was not about turning a buck; rather, it was about communicating the company's core, what made it authentic and pure. For Jobs, marketing was telling people what made Apple special. This is why Jobs loved it. It was an ongoing telling of what inspired Apple.

VIDEOS OF EMOTION: BALLOONS, SCULPTED CAMERA HOUSINGS, AND BREATHING BUBBLES

In this light, it makes sense why every product reveal by Apple is highlighted by clips showing the meticulous thought process that went into each device, including details that went into manufacturing the product. Who cares about how the widget is made? Just tell me about the bells and whistles. But that's not what Apple represents. It represents care, down to the screws it uses and cooling fans it installs. Hence, the company's website will post clips of how they make laptop casings out of a single block of aluminum or how their vision of a less "tangled" future is the inspiration behind the new generation of wireless ear buds.

Ads for the iPhone 7 entitled "Balloons" have no copy or text in it. There are no details on the size, weight, battery life, or cost of the phone. In fact, viewers don't even see the phone until the last 12 seconds of the clip.

And how does the website introduce the clip? It refers to it as a movie (even though it's only 1 minute long). In other words, it is a story.

A companion clip on the iPhone 7 has a voice-over from Jony Ive on the design approach used to improve the latest iteration of the blockbuster phone. In it, he talks about "sculpting the camera housing" and "making the antennae disappear" so that "each refinement serves to bring absolute unity and efficiency to the design." The clip, in essence, is a behind the scenes look at the obsessive attention Apple puts into their products.

The advertisement of Apple Watch (Series 2) took the same approach. There is minimal copy, only images and music that show the watch in a montage of scenes, punctuated by breathing bubbles, reminding the user to take deep breaths for sake of good health. It's all about connecting in a human way.

Then there is this paragraph describing the top-end version of the Apple Watch, which uses a ceramic housing:

> The process of creating the Apple Watch Edition case begins with a high-strength zirconia powder that's combined with alumina to achieve its rich, white color. Each case is then compression molded, sintered, and polished using a diamond slurry, which results in a remarkably smooth surface and an exquisite shine. With this precise level of workmanship, every Apple Watch Edition case takes days to make.[15]

Mixing zirconia powder with alumina? Cases are "sintered and polished using a diamond slurry?" What's sintered? A diamond slurry? Slurry is the language of snow cones and 7-Eleven drinks, not of diamonds? Isn't this an expensive way to do things? And then, "every Apple Watch Edition case takes *days* to make." Timex sells watches for $25, and Apple is making a case—not even the watch—that takes days to finish?

What's behind this kind of advertising? What's the thinking? It's the approach of "Here's what moves us." "This is our heart." It's the strategy of "Here's why we're here. If we deviate from this, we lose ourselves." Just look at the little booklet included in the box Apple Watch comes in—it has stitched binding. No staples allowed here. All this represents a commitment to staying true to the call. It's "how we win hearts." To further underscore the validity of the principle, look no further than Arkadi Kuhlmann. He proved the power of purity and congruency in the unlikeliest of industries.

THE ANTI-BANK BANK: ING DIRECT

"We are not a bank."[16] So began the rally cry that became ING Direct (Internationale Nederlanden Groep). It was a bank that would succeed wildly in becoming an anti-bank bank. Founded in 1996 against the backdrop of the dot-com bubble, ING Direct got its start in Canada, and within 6 months was able to attract 100,000 customers and its first billion dollars in deposits.[17] After 4 years, it pushed into the United States, and by 2008, ING would become the 21st largest bank in the United States (as ranked by deposits) and the number one direct online bank.[17] Seventy percent of Americans recognized the brand, and the company achieved the highest customer satisfaction rating among its industry peers.[18] On average, each and every day, customers would log on to their famous orange website 263,143 times and deposit over $47 million of savings.[17] By 2011, just before it was acquired by credit card powerhouse Capital One,[19] ING would become the 15th largest bank in the United States, with over $90 billion in assets and just under eight million in customers.[20] The results were staggering and undeniable. ING Direct had put the industry on notice.

How did ING Direct succeed so quickly in the staid and slow-moving industry of banking filled with behemoth players? How did this upstart company not only thrive but become an industry leader that many others would rush to copy?

FURY UNLEASHED

The root of ING's success can be traced to its founder and CEO, Arkadi Kuhlmann. He was hired by the Dutch conglomerate ING to see if he could expand the parent company's footprint into Canada.[21] At the time, Kuhlmann was only 33 years old but already a vice president at the Royal

Bank of Canada, the biggest of the country's "Big Five Banks."[22] Ironically, it was this insider experience that sowed the seeds of discontentment for Kuhlmann, as it would become the springboard for ING's radical strategy of becoming a new kind of bank, one that truly served customers instead of pillaging them.

In the words of Bruce Philp (CEO of marketing agency GWP, ING's marketing partner), Kuhlman spoke with the zeal of a revolutionary. Of their first encounter, Philip wrote

> [Kuhlmann] slapped a handful of competitive bank brochures down on the table the way an angry father might do with pornography he'd just found under his kid's bed. "Look at the fine print," he fumed, fanning the offending brochures out in front of him. "Who do they think they're in it for? You? Me? Their customers?"

> [He was outraged] by the paltry interest people got paid on their savings, while banks focused their marketing efforts on selling consumer debt. He railed against the usurious service charges people were forced to pay, the surly attention they received in return from their Soviet-esque bank branches and the similarly totalitarian lack of alternatives. The big banks were, by custom, by statute, by their own collective arrogance, all the same. ING Direct was almost a year away from actually launching in Canada, but Arkadi Kuhlmann was already trying to save the world.[23]

Kuhlmann was spitting mad and his fury was about to be unleashed. The vision was to right an institutional injustice and put banks on the side of the customer. Everything would revolve around doing right by the customer. He could care less about how the big banks did it. This was about caring for the little guy.

MAKING SAVINGS COOL

Kuhlmann's mission was to lead Americans back to savings. The mantra would be as simple and as clear as a church bell: "Save your money."

> "We [want] to cater to Main Street America, the 270 million Americans who are basically not getting a fair share. So, we [will] let the 9400 banks in

this country serve the 30 million rich Americans, and we [will] try to serve the 270 million on Main Street"[24]. The CEO would add, "Our purpose is to be a servant of the average person. Rather than getting people to spend more – which is what most banks do – our approach is to get Americans to save more – to return to the values of thrift, self-reliance, and building a nest egg."[25]

"The idea wasn't just a revolutionary business model, but a business model in service of a revolution."[26] Kuhlmann wanted to enable grandparents to save dollars so they could contribute to their grandkids' education, assist newlyweds to save up for their first house, or help enterprising young boys store up earnings from their first paper routes. Savings may have become a lost practice in the buy-crazy culture of America, but ING was going to help rekindle this most basic of life's disciplines. The idea was to make savings cool.[27] Savings spoke of self-reliance and independence. These were values that described Americans at their core. It would reso-nate with people instinctively and intuitively. The answer was to be an anti-bank bank.

A VIRTUAL BANK

The timing was right. With the digital revolution in full swing and Americans becoming used to using online tools, ING could exploit these new technologies by doing something radical—creating a bank in which there were no branches or buildings to walk into. It would be a virtual bank. The results would be seismic; by eliminating massive overhead expenses, ING was able to pass on its savings to customers by offering high-interest savings accounts.

ING paid a rate of 4.5% versus the average 0.46% rate at big banks.[28] This was victory in its highest form. It was sweet revenge against the institu-tional, monolithic banks who paid pittance, and it worked perfectly in driving people to ING. Word-of-mouth endorsements acted to swell the ranks of ING customers, accounting for 41% of new accounts opened,[29] with 18% of the new customers coming from other banks.[30] Typical banks spent $300 or more to acquire a customer. ING had to only spend $50.[30] ING not only had loyal customers, they had created an army of evangelists.

These metrics became the envy of the industry, and it was a clear manifestation that the revolution was working. Main Street was winning and Wall Street was losing.[31] Disruption had come.

MARKETING A REVOLUTION

Several key principles guided ING's marketing efforts:

1. All promotions had to appeal to the common man.
2. It had to communicate the battle cry of saving money.
3. It had to stir emotions of injustice experienced at the hands of the current banking state.
4. It had to reflect the ethos of Kuhlmann, the man who was behind this uprising.[32]

As a result, ING employed different "guerrilla tactics," using such devices as hot air balloon rides, free gas outreaches, and large parade-size cash cow floats, all emblazoned with ING's catchy and iconic bright orange ball logo.[33] One strategy was particularly delighting to Kuhlmann. Bike patrols wearing orange windbreakers would hit the streets of New York, Boston, Atlanta, Miami, and Los Angeles peddling the brand and message of ING using postcards while cheerfully passing out little orange boxes of Tic Tacs.[34] To Kuhlmann, this was quintessential ING. In his words,

> These Bike Patrols made a clear statement about who ING serves: "We will be for everyone," the Orange Code says, and the Bike Patrols proved we meant it. There was no target group, no segmentation, no proto-consumer – just people getting off a streetcar; regular folks. Anyone old enough to open a bank account, and with a dollar and a hunger for independence, was welcome to join us, and we weren't above taking it to the streets to tell them so.[35]

All these efforts acted to impress deeply into the minds of the public what ING was about—its mission, its rebel spirit, and its great anti-bank products. The tactics were visceral, tangible, and goofy but relatable and endearing. This was intentionally an "un-slick" strategy. It was meant to convey authenticity. It was tied to the very heart of the CEO and who he was. There was complete alignment and congruence of the company all the way back to the person of the founder.

HERE COMES SIMPLICITY

To execute on its mission, like Jobs and Apple, ING was committed to keeping things simple. Whenever and wherever they could simplify things, they did. Early on, Kuhlmann made it clear this strategy was imperative in creating a great customer experience. "We would make our products simple, allowing customers to save time and money. I really believed that this would challenge us every day to be an enterprise of continuous improvement."[36] ING would strive to make dealing with them as pleasurable as possible by making things easy and unencumbered. Consequently, the company offered "exactly one type of savings account and one type of checking account. Signing up online [took] five minutes, not much longer than a stop at McDonald's."[28] Whereas the typical process to opening a saving account involved 14 steps, ING reduced it to three.[30] This kind of result was exactly Kuhlmann's goal—to bring a McDonald's-like efficiency to ING. Kuhlman stated, "Suggesting there [was] a McDonald's approach to banking [was] heresy,"[28] to which Philp added

> Simplification, as obvious as it might seem in hindsight, has been one of ING Direct's most fundamental ways of saving the saver. The products themselves must be simple. The process of signing up must be simple. Simplicity is an invitation to customers not only to act, but to act with trust. Simple means nothing to hide.[37]

Simplicity paid dividends for everyone involved. Customers felt safe trying ING's services because they were uncomplicated, understandable, straightforward. People loved the absence of fine print, hand-waving, or hard-sell tactics. They felt like they could trust such a no-frills company, which in turn led them to entrust their money to ING. This was exactly the win–win scenario Kuhlmann hoped to create.

FIRING THE CUSTOMER: STAYING TRUE TO THE BRAND

To further burnish ING's contrarian ways, the company took on the "the customer is always right" maxim. Because ING had dedicated itself to a revolution of savings, the only way it could make good on the promise of high interest rates was to be ruthless in cutting costs in every way possible, even down to eliminating monthly printed account statements. Early on in the company, while manning the customer's lines as was Kuhlmann's practice, he took a call from a lady with a substantial balance at ING. She demanded that she be sent a printed statement, even invoking what she thought was the legal responsibility of ING to do so (it is not, banks are only required to issue year-end statements). As she kept on insisting it was the law to receive such a statement, "Kuhlmann lost his patience and snapped. That's it. You're not ready for this way of banking, and he closed her account."[38] The customer had been fired.

In building a company committed to savers, ING had a very defined picture of the customers it could serve and those it couldn't. Manager Omar Woodward stated, "Customers who don't fit our business model don't fit our business model and that's totally O.K."[28] Not every customer fits. As Kuhlmann would explain, "ING Direct is for everybody, but not everybody is for ING Direct."[38] If ING tried to become all things to all people, it would lose its value proposition, and dilute the power of its model. Kuhlmann showed great leadership by insisting on maintaining the purity of its approach. Sacrificing the model for a few ornery customers would have compromised the DNA of the company. Kuhlmann would have none of that. The CEO made sure the company stayed consistent to its mission, even to the point of firing a customer.

CONGRUENCE WINS BIG

ING was disruptive, innovative, and 100% focused on serving the people. As CEO, Kuhlmann exhibited a bee-inspired, straight-line desire to connect authentically and passionately with the average person on the street. Everything in between served that cause—marketing, operations, branding, executing, advertising, customer service, and more. It's a shining example on how to align everything organizationally to what you care about, and in ING's case, that came down to caring about one thing: righting a wrong—raging against low interest rates and leading people back to the good feelings of saving their money.

In the story about the Bike Patrols, one other detail brings home the spirit of ING. Kuhlmann was not only on the streets to witness the young fire-brands on wheels, he was in charge of pumping the tires, lubing the chains, and making sure the gears shifted properly.[34] It was a perfect snapshot of ING. The company's strategy was as charming, simple, and enduring as a bike, and its aspirations were as simple as helping people out. ING was a company about "pumping up people's tires." When that's what your company is about, you don't need to sell it. It sells itself.

ING is an inside-out story. It started with the founder's agitation, progressed to strategy and design, and then finished with an amazing bottom line. It began with a cause in the CEO's heart and ended with billions deposited in savings accounts all across America. If all companies were that clear about their purpose and that consistent in staying aligned to their cause, then more businesses would end up like ING and Apple because congruence wins big when companies go big on congruence.

 BOOT CAMP #8: STAYING TRUE

1. Name three tough decisions you made to stay true to the mission of your organizations.

2. Have you ever "left money (profits) on the table" in your pursuit of caring deeply? Was it worth it? If so, why?

3. Do you consider your organization to be congruent to its mission of care? If not, what's wrong and how can it be fixed? If it is congruent, can it be sharpened? How?

10

Continuity: Finding the Next Carer-in-Chief

He told me he had decided that I should be CEO.[1]

—**Tim Cook**

Apple has had five CEOs in its 40-year history. Besides Steve Jobs, only one has succeeded—the one Jobs chose. It could be argued that in addition to the great products Jobs is associated with, and the amazing company that Apple has become, his choosing of Tim Cook to succeed him as CEO is one of his greatest accomplishments.

Sequels, as convention says, are rarely better than the original. But in Jobs' case, he has pulled off the rare event of selecting a successor that has succeeded greatly.

The issue of appointing a successor is one of the most strategic and important decisions a CEO will ever make. Legacy depends on it. And while its importance is acknowledged, a Stanford study found an appalling lack of attention to this critical matter. A few alarming statistics from that study:[2]

1. More than 50% of 140 companies polled could not "immediately name a successor to their CEO should the need arise."
2. "A full 39% of respondents cited that they have zero viable internal candidates."
3. "On average, boards spend only 2 hours a year on CEO succession planning."
4. "Only 50% have a written document detailing the skills required for the next CEO."

Jobs, however, once again showed his leadership acumen by not only tending to what was necessary but doing it with great intentionality and thought. "For *years* he and other board members had insisted that Apple have a succession plan in place without disclosing what it was."[3] As Jobs passed through two serious bouts with his health in 2004 and 2009, the pace and weight of landing on a successor became more and more paramount. Finally, in 2011, as would turn out to be Jobs' third and last battle with pancreatic cancer, he sensed his time was near. It was time to turn over the keys. "As his health deteriorated throughout the summer, Jobs slowly began to face the inevitable: He would not be returning to Apple as CEO. So it was time for him to resign. He wrestled with the decision for weeks, discussing it with his wife, Bill Campbell, Jony Ive, and George Riley. 'One of the things I wanted to do for Apple was to set an example of how you do a transfer of power right.' He joked about all the rough transitions that had occurred at the company over the past thirty-five years. 'It's always been a drama, like a third-world country. Part of my goal has been to make Apple the world's best company, and having an orderly transition is key to that.'"[4]

As Jobs was facing his final hours, he understood that for disruption to continue, for the universe to experience more dents, and for more lives to be touched, the next leader had to be the next Carer-in-Chief, not just who could lead the next product cycle. Collectively, Sculley, Spindler, and Amelio nearly ran the company into the ground during Jobs' exile years. Now Jobs had the opportunity to personally appoint his own successor. As told by Cook,

> On August 11, [2011] a Sunday, Steve called Tim Cook and asked him to come over to the house. He said, "I want to talk to you about something," remembers Cook. This was when he was home all the time, and I asked when, and he said, "Now." So I came right over. He told me he had decided that I should be CEO. I thought then that he thought he was going to live a lot longer when he said this, because we got into a whole level of discussion about what would it mean for me to be CEO with him as a chairman. I asked him, "What do you really not want to do that you're doing?" "It was an interesting conversation," Cook says, with a wistful laugh. "He says, 'You make all the decisions.' I go, 'Wait. Let me ask you a question.' I tried to pick something that would incite him. So I said, 'You mean that if I review an ad and I like it, it should just run without your okay?' And he laughed, and said, 'Well, I hope you'd at least ask me!' I asked him two or three times,

'Are you sure you want to do this?' because I saw him getting better at that point in time. I went over there often during the week, and sometimes on the weekends. Every time I saw him he seemed to be getting better. He felt that way as well. Unfortunately, it didn't work out that way."[1]

Having told Cook personally that he was to succeed him, Jobs then told the board two weeks later on August 24. So ill was Jobs that he had to be transported to the board meeting by wheelchair. Once there and surrounded by the six outside directors,

He began to read aloud from a letter he had dictated and revised over the previous weeks. "I have always said if there ever came a day when I could no longer meet my duties and expectations as Apple's CEO, I would be the first to let you know," it began. "Unfortunately, that day has come." The letter was simple, direct, and only eight sentences long. In it he suggested that Cook replace him, and he offered to serve as chairman of the board. "I believe Apple's brightest and most innovative days are ahead of it."[5]

It was an emotional moment for the board. Each, one by one, recounted the incredible accomplishments of Jobs, many with tears in their eyes. Then the official resolutions were made. Tim Cook had become the next CEO of Apple.

Poignantly, as the meeting concluded with conversation about how HP had quit the tablet segment while competing against Apple, Jobs—who so revered HP as a young man—remarked with sadness,

"Hewlett and Packard built a great company, and they thought they had left it in good hands," he said. "But now it's being dismembered and destroyed. It's tragic. I hope I've left a stronger legacy so that will never happen at Apple."[5]

COOK: MORE THAN JUST TALENTED

In many ways, Cook was the obvious choice to be the next CEO. He had led Apple in 2004 and 2009 while Jobs was battling cancer and had done it with skill and steadiness. After being hired by Compaq in 1998 as a supply chain expert, Cook quickly began to show his mettle. When offered the opportunity to work at Apple, his initial instinct was to turn the job down.

Having spent 12 years at IBM and then moving on to Compaq, his career was one of respectability and achievement. But upon meeting Jobs, he, like so many others caught up in the whirlwind of the man, was drawn to a new world of possibilities:

> "Five minutes into my initial interview with Steve, I wanted to throw caution and logic to the wind and join Apple," he later said. "My intuition told me that joining Apple would be a once-in-a-lifetime opportunity to work for a creative genius. Engineers are taught to make a decision analytically, but there are times when relying on gut or intuition is most indispensable."[6]

Going with his gut, Cook would accept Jobs' offer to join the team. And for the next 15 years, it turned out to be a perfect complement for Jobs:

> Where Jobs was mercurial, Cook was calm. When Jobs cajoled, Cook implored. Jobs eviscerated volubly; Cook did so with so little emotion that one observer likened the experience to a dressing-down by a seething quiet parent: "You wished he'd scream instead and just get it over with." Jobs was larger than life; Cook faded into the woodwork. Jobs was the epitome of right-brain vision, Cook the embodiment of left-brain efficiency. Jobs bore the exotic Middle Eastern hues of his biological father and a kinetic aura that excited those around him. Cook is the prototypical Southerner: square-jawed, broad-shouldered, pale-skinned, with graying hair and an overall blandness to his appearance and demeanor. Jobs wore distinctive round spectacles. Cook wears barely noticeable clear, rimless glasses. Critically, Cook wasn't threatening to Jobs, there being no question who was the rock star and who was the bloke on bass guitar. Jobs' ego could tolerate Cook's rise because Cook's ego was impossible to discern.[7]

As an operational wizard and "ruthless systems guy," Cook had an uncanny ability to fix seemingly any problems in the organization.[8] "Cook was known for his prodigious memory and command of facts."[9] His mastery of details, particularly spreadsheets, was the stuff of legends. In long, detailed meetings, he would drill down and ask subordinates about the "variance on column d, line 514."[10] One coworker stated, "His ability to go from forty thousand feet to nose-against the windshield [was] amazing."[10]

Over time, like a vacuum cleaner, he swallowed up more and more responsibilities. Besides overseeing supply chain and inventory (in his early days, he famously cut Apple's suppliers from one hundred to twenty four, decreased company warehouses by half, and reduced inventory holds from 30 days to 6, to finally just 2 days[11]), Cook took over sales, then customer support, then Mac hardware, then negotiations with wireless carriers. Even Jobs admitted, "I'm a good negotiator, but he's probably better than me because he's a cool customer."[12] Cook was adding departments like David was collecting stones for his pouch. Finally, he was running the company on behalf of Jobs. Though Jobs was seen as superhuman, Cook had his own "superpowers."[13]

While Cook's world-class abilities were never in doubt, there were doubts if he could be Jobs' successor. Jobs' star shone so brightly next to Cook's humble, Southern quiet demeanor; it seemed he was the antithesis of Jobs. How would the outside world take to an "opposite" when so much of Apple's persona was built on Jobs' charisma? Cook stated, "Some people resent the fact that Steve gets credit for everything, but I've never given a rat's ass about that. Frankly speaking, I'd prefer my name never be in the paper."[12] Given his aversion to the spotlight and profile as a systems guy, many could not picture him as Apple's next leader:

> Right before Jobs stepped down for his 2009 medical leave, a prominent Silicon Valley investor who was unwilling to be quoted by name called the likelihood that Cook would become CEO "laughable," adding that "they don't need a guy who merely gets stuff done. They need a brilliant product guy, and Tim is not that guy. He is an ops guy."[14]

Even Jobs stated, "Tim's not a products guy,"[12] which seemed like quite an indictment against a key leader. Yet despite Jobs' assessment, this was not disqualifying in Jobs' mind. While it may have been true, Jobs saw there was a way forward for Apple that did not have to depend on a "products guy". What was it that Jobs saw in Cook that made him so appropriate to succeed Jobs? For all the operational prowess that Cook possessed, Jobs saw something others did not see. Cook cared deeply. Caring was the harder quality to come by. Not everyone had it. Not everyone got it. He had the X-factor Jobs was looking for. That is, his prodigious talent was matched by his love for Apple and what it stood for. He had fully assimilated Jobs' heart. He was the man.

PROOF IS IN THE PUDDING

Was Jobs' choice correct? Cook recently passed his fifth anniversary as CEO. And while there are spots for improvement, Cook's performance has been stellar. Statistically, he has had one of the best "successor" runs in business history. Consider the following numbers since Cook took over:[15-19]

The stock price has more than tripled from $54 to $155.

Revenues have doubled from $108 billion to $233 billion.

Apple sold its one billionth iPhone making it the greatest consumer product of all time, surpassing Playstation (382 million), Rubik's Cube (350 million), and Michael Jackson's music album (Thriller—70 million).

Apple Watch has become the most successful watch in the world, surpassing previous #1 Rolex.

Services have grown to $27 billion (a Fortune 100 company in itself).

Cash reserves of the company have grown to $230 billion—bigger than GDP of countries like Portugal and Hungary.

Stock buybacks: $127 billion.

Dividends: $44.8 billion distributed.

Named the most valuable company in the world since 2011.

Never before has a leader done so well in a successor role, and it's a testament to Cook's ability to execute the playbook like never before, except with much higher stakes. The weight of filling Jobs' shoes was hard to imagine. Without any hyperbole, it was the toughest act to follow in corporate history. So revered was Jobs that not a thing has been moved in his fourth floor corner office since his death; it's been left untouched. His name plate is still on the door. Cook says, "I literally think about him every day."[20]

Two years later in November 2013 at Laurene Powell's 50th birthday (Jobs' wife), John Lassetar, Pixar's head, shared,

I was at Laurene's birthday party, her fiftieth birthday, in San Francisco. I got there a bit early, and Tim came in. He came over and we started talking, and of course we started talking about Steve. I said, "Do you miss him? I really miss Steve." "And I showed him this," says Lassetar, pointing to the favorites list on his iPhone. "I still have Steve's number on my phone. I said, "I'll never be able to take that out." And Tim took out his iPhone and showed me—he still had Steve's number in his phone, too.[21]

The man who succeeded Jobs was a man that loved him dearly, so much so he offered his own liver to Jobs during Jobs' second bout with cancer. Jobs said no.[22]

THE STRATEGY BEHIND REMARKABLE: FOLLOWING STEVE AND NOT FOLLOWING STEVE

How has Cook achieved the remarkable and kept Apple at the forefront? Did he just ride a gravy train that was already set in motion by Jobs or did he have a strategy without which Apple could not have continued its winning ways? In a wide-ranging interview marking his fifth anniversary, Cook summarized his approach to leading Apple. It came down to three things: people, strategy, and execution. Befitting of Apple's penchant for simplicity and elegance, Cook distilled his leadership mandate to these three areas:

> I've got the best job in the world. I think about my day and weeks and months and years—I put them in three buckets: *people, strategy and execution.* I sort of move between those on a daily basis as to where I put my time. I always think the *most important one of those is people.* If you don't get that one right, it doesn't matter what kind of energy you have in the other two— it's not enough.[15]

Could leading the most valuable company in history be summarized so concisely? It seemed so. And noteworthy is how the three elements are linked in a strategic sequence. Execution (impact) cannot happen without strategy (roadmap), and strategy can't happen without good people (talent). In the previous section, it was seen how Cook executed and delivered at the highest levels. Five years is enough time to say there is a body of work by which Cook can be judged as "not just lucky" but as one that has stewarded Apple with tremendous skill. How did he accomplish this? Two key things can be discerned: he faithfully followed Steve, and he has faithfully not followed Steve.

Following Steve

In January 2009, while on a conference call with Wall Street analysts, Cook uncharacteristically went off script and provided a manifesto on Apple, which the press later dubbed the "Cook doctrine." It was a peek into what a Cook tenure would look like:

> We believe that we are on the face of the earth to make great products, and that's not changing. We are constantly focusing on innovating. We believe in the simple not the complex. We believe that we need to own and control the primary technologies behind the products that we make, and participate only in markets where we can make a significant contribution. We believe in saying no to thousands of projects, so that we can really focus on the few that are truly important and meaningful to us. We believe in deep collaboration and cross-pollination of our groups, which allow us to innovate in a way that others cannot. And frankly, we don't settle for anything less than excellence in every group in the company, and we have the self-honesty to admit when we're wrong and the courage to change. And I think, regardless of who is in what job, those values are so embedded in this company that Apple will do extremely well.[23]

These comments were stunning for its clarity, its conciseness, and its powerful declaration of what Apple would look like without Steve. Cook had not only assimilated the essence of Steve—his thinking, his heart, his passion, his values, his methods—he owned it. This was not an intellectual parroting of what Jobs cared about; it was a spontaneous manifesto of what he cared about. It was his creed. This was him. The way forward for Apple was to change nothing about Apple. It was to continue to bring life to Steve's spirit and vision.

On Cook's first day as CEO, he was true to his word from two years back when he sent a memo to all employees: "I want you to be confident that Apple is not going to change."[15] In this sense, keeping Apple remarkable was simple. Don't change a thing about the DNA. Just keep it going. Jobs' principles had proven themselves over and over. To tamper with it would have been stupid, tantamount to throwing away the recipe for the best chocolate cake in the world. Pursuant to Steve's values, what Cook refers to as Apple's immutable qualities, Cook vigilantly and passionately kept the company in line and on track with what made the company great. Some excerpts on how he has navigated the company:[15,24]

> "[Our] North Star has always been the same, which for us, is about making insanely great products that really change the world in some way—enrich people's lives."

"Our goal has never been to make the most. It's always been to make the best."

"We try to be as secretive as we've always been on products. We've always viewed that people love surprises."

"I don't subscribe to [the idea Apple is getting too big to grow] because it's traditional thinking in a lot of ways: You can't get large because you are large." (Disruptive, no limits mindset)

"Apple is the only company that can take hardware, software and services and integrate those into an experience that's an 'aha' for the customer."

"At the end of every board meeting, I discuss succession with the board because I might step off the wrong curb or something. We have the good discipline to do that. And I take that role extremely seriously."

"The ET [executive team] meeting has been going on at the same time on the same day for the 18-plus years I've been at the company, [even after Steve passed away]."

"The things that we do are bold. So we set out with bold objectives, but we proceed with care. And by care, I don't mean checking everything a hundred times before you do anything. I mean that you really care deeply about the details, because the details make the difference between a great product and a good or average product. That's what I mean by care. I wouldn't confuse caution and care."

That Cook has so fastidiously stewarded Steve's vision is a textbook example of what successors are called to do, namely, preserve institutional memory (defined as "lessons of organizational experience") so as to "ensure the continued effective performance of an organization" and "retain individual and knowledge capital for the future."[25] Part of Cook's success has been simple—just keep deploying the Jobsian template.

Not Following Steve

On the other hand, part of Cook's success has been not to follow Steve, just as Jobs advised Cook before he died:

"Never ask what I would do. Just do what's right." Jobs wanted Apple to avoid the trap that Walt Disney Co. fell into after the death of its iconic founder, Cook said, where "everyone spent all their time thinking and talking about what Walt would do."[26]

Taking those words to heart was the permission Cook needed to be his own man while honoring and continuing Jobs' precedence. Jobs was incredibly wise to unbind Cook from the crippling and onerous expectations he would have to bear if his mission was to be like Jobs. Cook stated, "To me, Steve's not replaceable. By anyone. He was an original of a species. I never viewed that was my role. I think it would have been a treacherous thing if I would have tried to do it."[15] Cook refers to those words—"Just do what's right"—as Jobs' greatest gift to him. "There's no bigger gift he could have given me than that statement. He took away the heavy weight."[15]

Since so much of Cook was already channeling Jobs, rarely did he have to look back and ask, "What would Steve do?" As a result, little by little, Apple has come to look like Cook without changing how it looked under Jobs. This was achieved by masterfully balancing the "immutables" of the company with the person that Cook is. Hence, Apple has taken on organizational initiatives and emphases not seen under Jobs.

Rewarding Shareholders

Jobs was well known for his distaste for paying dividends. Three primary reasons made it so. First, Jobs wanted cash on hand to make fast pivots when Apple needed to make acquisitions or invest quickly in product pushes. Second, he wanted to keep a margin of safety after Apple's near-bankruptcy experience in 1997. "The cash in the bank gives us tremendous security and flexibility."[27] Third, not issuing dividends saved the company 15% on taxes, which followed Warren Buffet's rationale with Berkshire Hathaway, which has not paid out dividends in 47 years; Buffet's strategy for utilizing cash reserves is to initiate stock buybacks.[28,29]

But as Apple's cash reserve ballooned to over $100 billion, Cook faced a mountain of money Jobs had never faced. And what felt right to him was to do something Jobs never did. On March 19, 2012, "Apple said it would pay its first dividend in 17 years and buy back $10 billion in stock."[15] Cook split the middle. He started paying dividends, but he also hedged against dividend taxes by initiating stock buybacks. Since 2012, Apple has paid nearly $50 billion in dividends and spent $117 billion in stock buybacks.[30]

Social Issues

Cook has famously made social issues a signature feature of his tenure, something Jobs was quiet on:

> I think everybody has to make their own decision about it. Maybe there are compelling reasons why some people want to be silent. I think for us, though—for a company that's all about empowering people through our products, and being a collection of people whose goal in life is to change the world for the better—it doesn't sit right with me that you have that kind of focus, but you're not making sure your carbon footprint isn't poisoning the place. Or that you're not evangelizing moving human rights forward. I think every generation has the responsibility to enlarge the meaning of human rights. I do view that a CEO today of Apple should participate in the national discussion on these type of issues.[15]

On the issue of human rights, despite his introversion and love for privacy, Cook came out as gay on October 30, 2014, in a Bloomberg Businessweek article. He is the first declared gay CEO of a Fortune 500 company.[15]

On the environment, as trumpeted by the company's website, Apple is passionately committed to a green future, pledging to using 100% renewable energy and stating, "Our planet deserves our best thinking."[31]

On the topic of diversity, Apple states, "The most innovative company must also be the most diverse." The company posts metrics on their progress as to how hiring and employee demographics are changing. "Creating a culture of inclusion" is serious business under Cook.[32]

Philanthropy

In the spirit of Bill Gates and Warren Buffet who have challenged the mega-rich to give away a majority of their wealth, Cook stated his intention to give away nearly all $800 million of his personal wealth to philanthropy.[33] While charitable giving is a private decision, nevertheless for Jobs, it was not a focus for him. Reputedly, he felt his best contribution to society was through building up Apple and his own family; hence, he didn't have time for philanthropy.[34] Again, Cook's practice departed from his mentor, especially when Cook had approved early on in his tenure matching charitable funds from Apple for its employees up to $10,000.[35]

Apple Watch: First New Product Launch Under Cook

In many ways, the launch of the Apple Watch on September 9, 2014, 3 years after Cook assumed the leadership of Apple, was the first acid test of his incumbency. Did he have the chops to bring to market a disruptive product in continuation of Apple's incredible run? After all, what the masses lusted after was Apple's creative products. Was Apple Watch the company's next hit? As it turned out, the answer was yes and no. Apple Watch quickly became the best digital wearable in the world and after just two years became the leader in worldwide sales for *all* watches by beating out Perennial #1 Rolex.[36] This was a considerable feat given the long-standing dominance of Swiss watches. However, revenues for the Watch are estimated to be in the $6.0 billion range.[19] Nothing to sneeze at but nothing compared to the giant revenues of iPhone, which pulls in over $140 billion annually.[15] On a percentage basis, Apple Watch generates only three percent of the revenue iPhone does. So while Apple Watch quickly ascended to the head of its class in wearables, again showing Apple's amazing ability to seize leadership wherever it goes, it was not the revenues hit of Apple's previous products. Apple Watch fit Cook's axiom, "Our goal has never been to make the most. It's always been to make the best."

Interestingly, while all eyes were on Apple Watch, it turned out Apple's services (iTunes, App Store, Apple Pay, iCloud, etc.) proved to be the "hidden hit" of Cook's tenure as it grew by a resounding $4 billion to over $23 billion in sales in one year, putting it in pace to become a Fortune 100 company just by itself.[15] Could it be that Apple's next hit was actually a service and not a product?

In either case, Cook's first product introduction was a hit in its category but not in terms of revenue (i.e., relative to other Apple products). Thus, the jury is still out as to whether Cook has a blockbuster in him or whether the blockbuster will be in an area not previously imagined. Despite the feeling among some analysts that Apple was losing its innovative edge, Fortune named Cook the world's greatest leader in 2015.[33]

MOVING THE DOT

But as stated by Cook, of the three pillars of his leadership, it's the people pillar that is the most important. "If you don't get that one right, it doesn't matter what kind of energy you have in the other two—it's not enough."[15]

This is where Cook's leadership has deviated most distinctly from Jobs.

Cook has moved the "people dot" from 1 to a 9. As viewed by what is arguably the best known (and deceptively simple) managerial model in academics—pioneered by Blake and McCanse in the early 1960s[37]—Cook has moved the dot from a 9,1 to a 9,9 in regard to balancing "concern for results" versus "concern for people." (Figure 10.1)

At the end of his life, all of Jobs' closest lieutenants spoke with the highest regard for Jobs' humanity and care as a person;[38] however, his leadership history showed that Jobs valued concern for results much more or at the

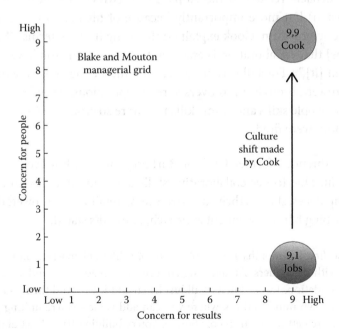

FIGURE 10.1
Blake–Mouton styles approach to leadership.

expense of concern for people. Cook has dramatically changed this. Cook has elevated the concern for people without compromising the concern for results. This is a distinguishing mark of Cook's leadership.

Anecdotally, as shared by Eddy Cue, Sr. VP of Internet software and services, who reported to Jobs first and now reports to Cook,

> I twitch less, says Cue cheerfully when I ask about the difference between Jobs and Cook. "No, no, no, just kidding! Steve was in your face, screaming, and Tim is more quiet, more cerebral in his approach. When you disappoint Tim, even though he isn't screaming at you, you get the same feeling. I never wanted to disappoint Steve, and I never want to disappoint Tim."[39]

Besides the fundamental tonal change, Cook has also reinforced the collaboration and chemistry piece that is critical to how Apple operates. One of Cook's first high-profile firings was Scott Forstall, a rising star under Jobs and reputed to have been a successor candidate. Forstall was let go for the debacle related to the Apple Maps (which was under Forstall's supervision) but more importantly because of his inability to get along with the senior team. Cook explained the firing in these terms, "My deep belief [is] that collaboration is essential for innovation. You have to be an A-plus at [it]."[40] Forstall was not an A-plus and neither was an early hire, John Browett, brought in to oversee retail operations. They both did not have the people skills and team skills that were so crucial to Cook's people pillar. Both were fired.

Angela Ahrendts, former CEO of Burberry, proved, however, to be the perfect fit. Due to her collaborative skills and natural ability to connect with employees, she has thrived in overseeing retail where Browett did not. In describing her management approach, Ahrendts stated,

> In the first six months I was able to hit 40 different markets and spend time with the leaders. An amazing culture was already built and an amazing foundation. I would first of all just listen and learn. And then you start in your own mind to think where you can add value—you're uniting people, you're getting them to collaborate. You're building trust. That alone is empowering.[41]

Tellingly, retention rates at Apple Stores hit an all-time high of 88% under Ahrendts.[41] People matter, and executives with people skills matter greatly to Cook.

Additionally, unlike Jobs, Cook has allowed his senior managers to publically carry more of Apple's message and to represent Apple in various media outlets (e.g., The New Yorker, Fast Company, Fortune, Bloomberg). This is part of Cook's strategy to be more transparent and to do so by sharing Apple's key executives with the world. He trusts them. "My objective is to raise the public profile of several of the folks on the executive team, and others as well. Because I think that's good for Apple at the end of the day."[33] That's good for Apple because for Cook, it broadens the people and human connection to the company, which underscores Cook's charming engineer-speak when he says, "the most important data points are people."[33]

Five years after Jobs passing, Apple is not just surviving; it's thriving. The continuity has been remarkable for its smoothness and uninterrupted sense of mission and impact. Jobs did himself well when he choose Apple's next CEO not based on conventional wisdom—that the person had to be a "products guy"—but based on one who would carry on Apple's name with passion and commitment as a result of his deep care. Jobs passed one of the greatest tests of a leader. It turns out choosing Tim Cook was Apple's next big hit.

BOOT CAMP #9: DEVELOPING NEXT-GEN LEADERS

1. Jobs chose Cook not only on the basis of competency but on Cook's ownership of Apple's mission of care. Do you think Jobs has succeeded in passing on Apple's greatest asset through Tim Cook? Why or why not?

2. If you die today, who will lead your company?

3. How are you preparing your successor? Jobs spent much personal time (years) working with and mentoring Cook. Do you have a personal mentoring strategy? If so, what is it? If not, why not?

Section IV

Activation

11

Canvas:
Putting Caring Deeply to Work

THE *BETTER* LEADERSHIP CANVAS

To assimilate the lessons in this book, a leadership canvas is presented as follows. It's designed to spur application and personalization. It's an exhortation to action. By utilizing the word "better," the core ideas of caring deeply are brought to life by associating them with nine corresponding leadership identities. Previously, at each chapter's end, "boot camps" were presented to spur thoughts that connect to the *Better* leadership canvas. These boot camps served as primers to making the concepts in the disruptive leadership model practical and actionable (Figure 11.1).

Key points from each previous chapter are reviewed through the use of this canvas. As you work through this canvas, you may well find this to be the most important chapter of the book, as no disruptive leadership can show itself without new leadership behavior.

LEADERSHIP IDENTITY #1: BE ON A MISSION OF CARE

How Can I Make the World *Better?* (Caring Deeply)

Everyone is created to care deeply. Everyone has a "caring deeply" gene. It's what gives meaning to life. It's been said the two most important days of a person's life are when he is born and when he finds out the reason why he was born. When a person finds that, their life moves to a different plane. It's a plane of meaning and contribution. It also means there is now the capacity to *Better* the world. One has the sure foundation to be a reformer.

The *Better* Leadership Canvas: Creating your roadmap to impact
Nine leadership identities in the Disruptive Leadership Model

Leadership	Organization	Global impact
Caring deeply	Core team	Commitment
1. Be on a mission of care How can I make the world *Better*? (Pursuing excellence)	**4. Be a mobilizer** Finding those who will do *Better* with me (Recruiting talent)	**7. Be strong and courageous** Having the fortitude to achieve *Better* (Execution and follow-through)
Clarity	Culture	Congruency
2. Be a visionary This is what *Better* looks like (Goal-setting)	**5. Be a social architect** How will I nurture *Better* as a community? (Core values)	**8. Be uncompromising** Protecting the mission of *Better* (Staying true)
Credibility	Creativity	Continuity
3. Be the best at one thing Continually growing myself to be *Better* (Personal development)	**6. Be an innovator** Doing *Better* with genius (New thinking)	**9. Be succession-savvy** Appointing the next leader in *Better* (Developing next-gen leaders)
I. Eruption ➡	II. Construction ➡	III. Disruption

FIGURE 11.1
The *Better* Leadership Canvas (BLC)—Kao, 2016.

How care is expressed will vary from individual to individual. This is what makes the world such a wonderful place. Each person is expressing that which animates and motivates him deeply. The nodes of care are as vast as the human experience. Everyone needs to find their node because therein lies his or her ability to be a leader of significance.

Steve Jobs was a man deeply moved and deeply captivated by beauty and simplicity, and how that could be brought to bear on technology and the liberal arts. His passion was to make products that could move the world forward. His vision was to make a dent in the universe, or as Harvard graduate Donovan Livingston put it, to leave a crater, which reminds us that "something amazing happened here."

Introspection

What do you care about? Not just in the normal sense, but in a revolutionary sense? What agitates you or inflames you? What captivates you or mesmerizes you? What makes you laugh or sing or cry? What triggers pain or pleasure? What grabs you so deeply that you would do it without getting paid? When work becomes play, then that's a signal you're getting close. As Tony Hsieh of Zappos asks, "What would you be passionate about doing for 10 years even if you never made a dime?"[1] The answers to these questions don't necessarily come overnight, but when they do, there is a blinding effect. This is it. This is what I was born for.

Jotting It Down

The path to revelation and revolution comes in a series of fragments, key words, or phrases that finally coalesce. Write down your thoughts, the little bullets of insight that beg to be explored and clarified. Or maybe, you've already nailed what you care deeply about and can devote your life to it. In either case, write, scribble, or diagram your passion; or alternatively zero in on one of the specific questions mentioned previously.

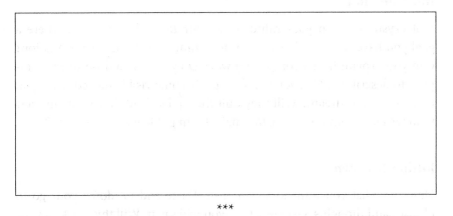

***

LEADERSHIP IDENTITY #2: BE A VISIONARY

This is What *Better* Looks Like (Clarity).

World-changing action can only be precipitated by world-changing ideas. This is what excites people, moves their hearts, and fires their imagination. It's what motivates them to sacrifice, dedication, and to take on the impossible.

Steve Jobs was a master motivator because his vision of *Better* was so clear. Technology in service of the arts was what would make the world a better place. Thus, products had to be taken to new heights. They had to be "insanely great." Doing so would be to "send ripples through the universe" and "invent the future." To settle for anything less was to settle for the mundane. The call was to be "pirates."

Danny Meyer of Union Square Cafe had equal clarity about the restaurant business. It wasn't about serving food. It was about hospitality, a hospitality rooted in the human heart that was defined at birth. "Within moments of being born, most babies find themselves receiving the first four gifts of life: eye contact, a smile, a hug, and some food. We receive many other gifts in a lifetime, but few can ever surpass those first four. That first time may be the purest 'hospitality transaction' we'll ever have."[2] What a crazy insight and what pure genius it was to build a restaurant empire upon it. Meyer's take on *Better* was out of this world fantastic.

Introspection

Is it crystal clear in your mind what your *Better* looks like? Is there a goal you have that people will want to commit to? What is your mission? Can you explain it in a compelling way? Do you have a drop-dead metaphor to describe it? Can you tell if people become visibly moved when you talk about your dream? Will they quit their jobs? Will they pony up their money? Does your take on *Better* make them giddy with excitement?

Jotting It Down

Describe what you want to accomplish. Write and jot down your go-to phrases and thoughts. Get clear how you will say it. Will this work as your elevator speech? Does it have a rallying effect?

***

LEADERSHIP IDENTITY #3: BE THE BEST AT ONE THING

Continually Growing Myself to be *Better* (Credibility)

Followership depends on credibility. Vision is necessary. Clarity is necessary. But for followers to follow, they need to know there is substance to their leader. He must be "best in class" in some area of his leadership. He must be an "outlier." Without it, followers will not have confidence that the requisite skills are in their leader to make the mission happen. This requires that the leader be committed to a continual process of renewal through learning, practice, mentoring, and openness. Jobs was described as possessing leadership abilities that were "fueled to an unusual degree by his unique gift for being an autodidact."[3] Jobs was a ferocious learner, aggregator, and synthesizer of information. Apple was continuously on the cutting edge because Jobs was always improving himself. Disruptive leaders can't lead disruptive companies without disrupting themselves. Ingvar Kamprad exhibited an uncanny ability to read consumer trends and exploit them for the common person to deliver the best value in furniture wares. Kamprad models the IKEA creed of frugality by living simply despite being a billionaire. He is a savant in saving and lives what he preaches. He is the ultimate in credibility.

Introspection

What skills or qualities do you have that set you apart? Do you have technical, human, or conceptual skills that place you above the crowd? Are you given to continuous learning? Do you have a track record of people following you? What are people attracted to in you? If you polled them, what reasons would they give for following you? Have you identified these qualities or abilities before? Do you have a plan to grow and extend yourself as a leader? Have you experienced plateaus? How did you break through?

Jotting It Down

Write down answers to the questions given earlier or thoughts triggered by them. Describe your qualifications. Don't be shy about what makes you unique and eminently worth following.

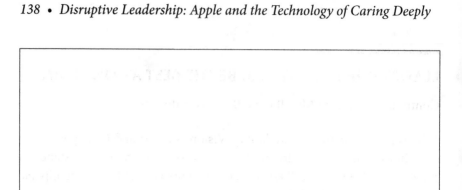

***

LEADERSHIP IDENTITY #4: BE A MOBILIZER

Finding Those Who Will Do *Better* with Me (Core Team)

There are few things in life more enjoyable than changing the world with friends. This is certainly part of the "joy in the journey." When you do amazing work with your buddies, the camaraderie itself is a reward. Being disruptive requires great teams. Leaders looking to make a difference must be strategic and intentional about building a core team—one that complements each other, sharpens, and above all can stand shoulder-to-shoulder together in battle. Unity of heart and mind are essential. This is not to say building teams is about surrounding oneself with yes men. Both Jobs and Phil Knight of Nike built incredible teams, but it didn't mean those teams were just rubber stamps to everything their leader said. On the contrary, these teams were marked by vigorous discussion, dissension, and shouting matches. Yet love (if it can be said) was the glue that kept them together and moving forward. As a disruptive leader, you must be able to mobilize and recruit. You must have an eye for talent. You must have a sense for who will enhance and multiply the impact of your team. It's one of your most important jobs.

Introspection

Have you built a team before? What did you do right? What did you do wrong? Did your assessment of people turn out correct or incorrect? When you evaluate people, do you have a bias or blind spot you need to be careful of? What kinds of things have your teams accomplished? Do your teammates exhibit great loyalty? (This is a measure of their "love" for you). Building a world-class team may be a once in a lifetime exercise because once it's formed, you may stay together forever. Do you have people you want to recruit now?

Jotting It Down

Describe what you want your team to look like and whom you want on your A-team. Jot down answers and phrases to the questions given earlier. Dream up your best team. Think through your friends list. Start with one person and build from there.

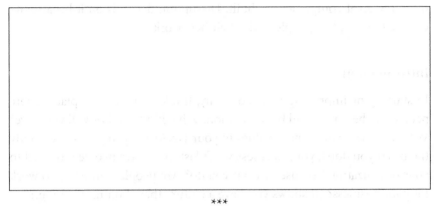

***

LEADERSHIP IDENTITY #5: BE A SOCIAL ARCHITECT

How Will I Nurture *Better* as a Community? (Culture)

Culture is about creating the soil that will let everyone flourish. It's architecting what your company will be. What does it stand for? What won't it tolerate? What is expected of people? How will things be done around here? Culture is about the outward "artifacts" and inward values. Will we be casual or buttoned down? Will we have open working spaces or be office-centric? Will we have free meals and massages? What is the management style here? Autocratic? Consensus? What are the values that drive this company? What do we hold to be our "immutable" values?

Of late, the culture of a company has become an intense focus of researchers and academics. More and more, experts point to and data substantiates that culture is a key to creating successful enterprises. Increasingly, people don't just see work as a place to get a paycheck; rather, it's about creating meaning, being part of a cause. Is this a place I can belong to because I believe in what this company is about?

In founding Apple, Jobs made meaning the #1 reason for its existence. When Zappos created a new way of selling shoes, it wasn't about shipping as many units as possible; it was about delighting customers with great service—delivering happiness. Zappos doesn't hire anyone unless they pass the "bus test." Were the applicants kind to the bus driver on the last leg home? The importance of culture has become a whole new realm of insight into how great companies are built. Disruption depends on it because it's culture that inspires people to do their best work.

Introspection

In starting or improving your company, think of building a place where people can belong to and be on mission. What kind of ethos will you have? What are the revolutionary values in your DNA? Do you yourself embody them? (If you don't, your business won't last long). Are people attracted to your organization because of what you do? Are people clamoring to work for your business? (It shows you have a culture that's humming along.)

Jotting It Down

Describe who you are, your values, and how that will determine how your organizational culture will look. Write down answers, phrases, fragments to the aforementioned questions. Do you have a model culture that inspires you? That can provide a starting point.

***

LEADERSHIP IDENTITY #6: BE AN INNOVATOR

Doing *Better* with Genius (Creativity)

In a sea of look-alikes, innovation is the great differentiator. It's what makes a company stand out; thus, the rally cry trumpeted in book after book, "innovate or die." Interestingly, Apple's approach to disruption has not been to be first to the market. It wasn't the first in the MP3 space. It wasn't the first smartphone maker. It wasn't the first tablet maker. Nor was it a first mover in the wearable market. Instead, they looked at the offerings in these segments and said these categories were ripe for disruption because they lacked creativity and panache, because the products were not designed with people in mind. There was little or no human connection built into them. This is where Apple has excelled with unparalleled impact. They've given the world products with unimaginable simplicity and elegance. Their products make human sense. Creativity and ingenuity make for companies that last and last, and lead their industry peers; enter 3M, the 114-year-old company that keeps on ticking. Why? Because innovation has been built into the center of its culture. The company is more inventors than managers. They are constantly coming up with new ways to do things—ways that are filled with ingenuity and insight.

Introspection

Are you an outside-the-box thinker? Do you delight in strategizing how to delight the customer? Are you constantly noodling and angling how to make things better? Do you have a nose for impressive simplicity and elegance? Are you driven by human-centric design? Genius has its moment of inspiration, but it is born of hard work, iterations, and prototyping. The spoils don't go to the lucky; they go to the prepared. Do you have an instinct, a relentless drive to surprise the world with crazy, good solutions? The ability to do *Better* with genius is an X-factor in disruptive companies. It's part of the secret sauce.

Jotting It Down

Describe your innovative impulses. Using the questions given earlier, write down phrases and sentences that describe your ability to be creative.

Think back on your track record. Write down how you've solved things in a novel way. Recall people who have been served by your creative solutions and what their reactions were.

*** ***

LEADERSHIP IDENTITY #7: BE STRONG AND COURAGEOUS

Having the Fortitude to Achieve *Better* (Commitment)

Do you have an iron gut? In your pursuit of *Better*, are you strong as steel and determined as hell? There will be surprises, difficulties, and even enemies. Leaders need to have fortitude—they must be strong and courageous. This is where the gut checks come in. How much do I believe in *Better*? How much will I sacrifice to achieve it? Am I good to see this to the end? Will I execute?

Part of Jobs' talent was his total commitment to "ship." *Better* wasn't done until it shipped—no matter how high the mountain that needed to be scaled. For disruption to happen, *Better* had to be delivered. Howard Schultz, in building Starbucks in its early days, faced innumerable mountains—from securing capital to overcoming unsupportive partners to beating back traitorous board members. It was hell. As Schultz would remark, Starbucks' success "is as much one of perseverance and drive as it is of talent and luck."[4] Every race starts out glorious, but does it end glorious? Everyone can look good out of the blocks, but can they make it to the end? Disruptive leaders are finishers and executors. They need not only skill to do that, they also need inner strength. No falling out. No aborted plans.

Introspection

What kinds of things have you had to overcome in life? What's the most extreme thing you've experienced and survived? Have there been situations where you've cracked or buckled? How did you remedy it? Are you a fighter? Do you have a stubborn streak that's warranted? Have you ever outlasted someone else to win something? Have you ever accomplished something when everyone else doubted? In leading an organization, can you rally the troops to make it through tough times?

Jotting It Down

Describe your acts of valor. Strength and courage are your insurance policy. The house may be burning down. The floods may be coming, but you will prevail. Your inner timber is crucial for you and your organization. People are given to fear and doubt. As a leader, you counter it with the opposite emotions. Rate your fortitude level on a scale of 1–10. In times of difficulty, where do you turn to for strength?

***

LEADERSHIP IDENTITY #8: BE UNCOMPROMISING

Be Uncompromising: Protecting the Mission of *Better* (Congruency)

While leading an organization can look like a straight-line proposition on paper, the reality is it's a zigzag. Navigating failures and success can cloud the mission. Detours can end up being the main road. It can be easy to lose the forest for the trees and forget where one's "North Star" is. One of the most important functions of a leader is to stay true to the mission. The pursuit of *Better* cannot be compromised.

Jobs was famous for keeping Apple on point. Mastering the art of refusal, Jobs embraced the "discipline of no" and defined strategy as "figuring out what *not* to do."[5] For Jobs, the reason for Apple's existence was always in view, and thus he protected the company from deviating. This a tribute to Jobs' restraint and self-control as he stated frequently, "I'm as proud of the products that we have not done as I am of the ones we have done."[6]

ING founder Arkadi Kuhlmann was also a master at staying the course and as a result built a powerhouse anti-bank bank by sticking to its guiding principle star of helping people save money. Everything in the company was aligned with that one idea. Everything was executed in concert with that mission. Kuhlmann's insistence and uncompromising stance helped ING change the banking industry.

Introspection

Are you good at staying on track? Are you good at not losing sight of the big picture? Have you had to be ruthless in cutting things or saying no to things? Are you adroit at prioritizing and making sure the unimportant doesn't distract from the important? Do choices paralyze you, or do you enjoy paring things down to clear the clutter? Have you been tempted to say yes to something because it would make money, even though it would be a deviation to the business? Are your values strong enough to make you walk away from money and profits?

Jotting It Down

Describe your ability to focus and prioritize. Write down examples where you've led a group to staying on track. Write down examples where you allowed your organization to go sideways. Which tendency outweighed the other?. List examples where you have turned down money to stay the course.

```



```

***

LEADERSHIP IDENTITY #9: BE SUCCESSION-SAVVY

Appointing the Next Leader in *Better* (Continuity)

There can be no legacy without an appropriate successor. The true impact of a leader's dream is whether it can live on past him. Certainly, the impact he makes with his own life is a huge accomplishment. But if the company can continue to the next generation and the next, then something magical has been established. The ability to create generational impact rests in upon the successors—those crossover points where the company is handed off to the next leader. For Apple, the passing of the baton from Steve Jobs to Tim Cook was the first successor transition since the company was founded in 1976. Not unlike the appointment of a new pope, observers were watching with keen interest for the "white smoke." But Jobs had taken all the drama out of it—on purpose. He didn't want any more boardroom shenanigans that had marked his years of exile. A world-class company needed to model a smooth transition, and that's exactly what happened. The appointment of Tim Cook nevertheless was somewhat unexpected because he was not in the charismatic mold of Jobs or a "products" guy like Jobs. But the world underestimated Jobs' wisdom. Jobs didn't need a "products" guy to lead the company; he needed someone who completely and thoroughly understood the essence and DNA of Apple. That man was Cook. If Apple was to endure, it would endure through its values, not through another person mimicking Jobs. Jobs' choice was full of wisdom. Enduring companies don't carry on through personalities; they carry on through their founding principles of care.

Introspection

When it's your turn to appoint a successor, what criteria will you use? Will it be based on personality? On gifting? On public opinion? Companies that endure are rare. Even rarer are companies that disrupt. But they are the most prized. Your leadership legacy depends not only on you succeeding but your successor succeeding, and the successor's successor succeeding. What's the best way to choose? Find someone that will honor and be faithful to the values that made the company great in the first place.

Jotting It Down

Write down the values that are most important to you in a successor. Keep a short list of potential candidates. Observe them over time. Which one naturally embodies the values and mission of the company while having the skill and aptitude to navigate future scenarios that will undoubtedly face the company? Choose wisely.

***

Putting It All Together: Storyboarding

Using your boot camp answers from previous chapters and canvas notes from above, bring it all together by writing your disruption story. This becomes your manifesto of care. It will provide the compass and know-how by which you operate as a leader and how to lead your organization. As time goes on, your story can be edited and updated, but get started by creating an initial narrative.

The following is an example:

1. **Caring deeply** (How I can make the world *Better*)—My dad was a war veteran. When he came back from serving, he was a different person. Post-traumatic stress syndrome overtook his life. Our family so looked forward to having him back, but we lost him. Our family was never the same.
2. **Clarity** (This is what *Better* looks like.)—I never want families to go through what I did. The government provided some help but not enough. I want to create a marketplace solution to help our men in uniform recover so they can enjoy productive lives again.
3. **Credibility** (Continually growing myself to be *Better)*—I've never been in war or served in the military, but I put myself through university and then went on to get my MBA through merit scholarships. Given my life story, I have a passion to use my learning and business skills to start something unique.
4. **Core team** (Finding those who will do *Better* with me)—I'm looking to recruit other talented business people that have had my same experience with their war dads. One of my good friends' father got blinded by a bomb blast. He's all in, and he's connected to venture money.
5. **Culture** (How I will nurture *Better* as a company)—We will establish a culture of honor, tenacity, and dignity to restore the men who have served to a place of wholeness, usefulness, and self-regard.
6. **Creativity** (Doing *Better* with genius)—We are part of the millennial techno-savvy generation. We will use all digital platforms available to us (e.g., apps, tablets, and trackers married with traditional counseling methodologies) to create a holistic solution. We will do everything in our power to come up with cutting-edge therapies.

7. **Commitment** (Having the fortitude to achieve *Better*)—We will not stop in our mission to help until we see whole cohorts recover with 90% success rates. Then we will share these solutions with other countries around the world that seek to mainstream their veterans back into society and into their nuclear family.

8. **Congruency** (Protecting the mission of *Better*)—This is a life's work. The impact it can have on families for generations to come is inestimable. Kids get their dads back. Wives get their husbands back. Grandchildren get to enjoy their grandparents. We will not deviate from our mission.

9. **Continuity** (Appointing the next leader in *Better*)—We are only on the front end of this company start-up, but my successor will clearly emerge as we labor to make this mission come to reality.

Use the blank canvas (Figure 11.2) to fill in your disruption story. Be succinct.

With this canvas, you have a "personal crib sheet" for being a disruptive leader. It will help you call to mind the key elements of how to harness your

My *Better* Leadership Canvas

Leadership		Organization		Global impact	
Be on a mission of care. How I plan to make the world *Better*...	Caring deeply	**Be a mobilizer.** Those who will do *Better* with me are...	Core team	**Be strong and courageous.** My exploits in achieving *Better*...	Commitment
Be a visionary. What my *Better* looks like...	Clarity	**Be a social architect.** I will nurture *Better* as a community by...	Culture	**Be uncompromising.** I'm determined to protect the mission of *Better* because...	Congruency
Be the best at one thing. How I'm growing myself to take on *Better*...	Credibility	**Be an innovator.** How I will do *Better* with genius...	Creativity	**Be succession-savvy.** My short list of the next leaders in *Better*...	Continuity
Eruption		Construction		Disruption	

FIGURE 11.2
Fillable leadership canvas.

technology of care in creating an organization of excellence and impact. Use this canvas to your advantage.

CONCLUSION: TAKING NOMINATIONS—HALL OF FAME

The soft stuff is the hardest stuff for competitors to copy.[7]

—Author Dr. Soren Kaplan

The things you care deeply about as a leader is your greatest competitive edge.

It's not something that can be easily copied or reproduced. No matter how many companies try to emulate Apple, they can never achieve Apple's success because their caring can never match Apple's. The best way to create disruption and make the world better is to find what you care about most. This is what Danny Meyer, Ingvar Kamprad, Phil Knight, Tony Hsieh, William McKnight, Howard Schultz, and Arkadi Kuhlmann did. They represent an amazing cast of Hall of Fame disruptors.

Of course, there are many other outstanding leaders that could have been profiled—many known, others not. But the most exciting part is membership to the "Hall" is not closed. It's ongoing and is always taking nominations. This generation's disruptors are looking for the next generation of disruptors. The world is waiting for the next iteration of leaders to show their creativity, determination, and pluck. Every act of disruption is another story of how the remarkable happens. But the extent to which the world can be bettered depends above all on how *deeply people care.* Apathy is the great enemy of progress. No matter how talented or brilliant a person is, if there is no care, there is no motivation to act. That's why it's the secret to change. Building a world-changing organization is a deeply human act.

It's been said, "Championships are won when no one is watching." That's a great encapsulation of the work of caring deeply. Breakthrough doesn't happen overnight or by happenstance. It is the result of focus, perseverance, smarts, collaboration, and skill. It all percolates and bakes while no one is looking. Disruption is 90% invisible and 10% visible. A turkey dinner can take 8–10 hours to make, but only 1 hour to be eaten. But what memories it creates, and how people keep coming back for more. Being a disruptor and building a great organization is like that. Put in the love, sweat, and tears and the payoff will be incredible. So go make some dents. Go leave a crater and show the world you care. What are you waiting for? The world is waiting on you.

References

INTRODUCTION

1. Elmer-De-Witt, P. (2017, September 12). Live from the Steve Jobs theater. *Apple 3.0.* Retrieved from https://www.ped30.com/2017/09/12/apple-view-cheap-seats/.
2. Honan, M. (2012, October 5). Why we'll never stop talking about Steve Jobs. *Wired.* Retrieved from http://www.wired.com/gadgetlab/2012/10/what-we-talk-about-when-we-talk-about-steve-jobs/.
3. Goldman, D. (2012, August 20). Apple is now the most valuable company of all time. *CNNMoney.* Retrieved from http://money.cnn.com/2012/08/20/technology/apple-most-valuable-company/index.htmlGo.
4. Kosoff, M. (2015, October 30). 11 mind-blowing facts about Apple that show just how massive the company really is. *Business Insider.* Retrieved from http://www.businessinsider.com/crazy-facts-about-apple-2015-10.
5. Panzarino, M. (2012, August 29). Apple now bigger by market cap than Microsoft, Google, Amazon and Facebook Combined. *The Next Web.* Retrieved from http://thenextweb.com/shareables/2012/08/29/apple-now-bigger-market-cap-microsoft-google-amazon-facebook-combined/.
6. Yglesias, M. (2012, September 22). Apple's market cap is bigger than all of Greece, Spain, Portugal, and Ireland put together. *Slate.* Retrieved from http://www.slate.com/blogs/moneybox/2012/09/22/apple_s_market_cap_bigger_than_the_combined_value_of_every_company_in_greece_spain_portugal_and_ireland_together_.html.
7. Emerson, R. and Smith, C. (2012, January 26). Apple's cash on hand: 9 things the company could pay for. *Huffington Post.* Retrieved from http://www.huffingtonpost.com/2012/01/24/apples-cash-on-hand_n_1229529.html.
8. Whitney, L. (2013, June 4). Apple to reach 600 million users by end of 2013, says analyst. *CNet.* Retrieved from http://news.cnet.com/8301-13579_3-57587517-37/apple-to-reach-600-million-users-by-end-of-2013-says-analyst/.
9. Leswing, K. (2016, April 4). Investors are overlooking Apple's next $50 billion business. *Business Insider.* Retrieved from http://www.businessinsider.com/credit-suisse-estimates-588-million-apple-users-2016-4.
10. Hackman, M.Z. and Johnson, C.E. (2009). Leadership: A Communication Perspective. Long Grove, IL: Waveland Press, Inc.
11. Christensen, C.M. (1997). The Innovators Dilemma. New York: HarperCollins.
12. United States Department of Labor (2015, January 1). Entrepreneurship and the U.S. Economy. *Bureau of Labor Statistics.* Retrieved from http://www.bls.gov/bdm/entrepreneurship/bdm_chart3.htm.
13. Wagner, E.T. (2013, September 12). Five reasons 8 out of 10 businesses fail. *Forbes.* Retrieved from http://www.forbes.com/sites/ericwagner/2013/09/12/five-reasons-8-out-of-10-businesses-fail/#a76d4c5e3c66.

CHAPTER 1

1. Walter, E. (2013, October 8). 5 myths of leadership. *Forbes*. Retrieved from http://www.forbes.com/sites/ekaterinawalter/2013/10/08/5-myths-of-leadership/#3473e301584b.
2. Schlender, B. and Tetzeli, R. (2015). Becoming Steve Jobs. New York: Crown Business, p. 45.
3. NASB (1999). The Holy Bible—New American Standard Bible. Grand Rapids, MI: Zondervan, I Sam. 17:26.
4. I Sam. 17:1–54.
5. Hoffner, H., Jr. (1968). A hittite analogue to the David and Goliath contest of champions? The Catholic Biblical Quarterly 30, 220–225.
6. I Sam. 17:26.
7. I Sam. 17:37.
8. I Sam. 8:5.
9. I Sam. 8:20.
10. I Sam. 11, 15.
11. Beck, J.A. (2006). David and Goliath, A Story of Place: The Narrative-Geographical Shaping of 1 Samuel 17. Westminster Theological Journal 68, 321–330.
12. I Sam. 16:12.
13. Isaacson, W. (2011). Steve Jobs. New York: Simon & Schuster, p. 443.
14. I Sam. 13:14.
15. Gladwell, M. (2008). Outliers—The Story of Success. New York: Little, Brown and Company.
16. MacLeod, H. (2004). *Leadership Is Easy.* Retrieved July 5, 2011, from www.gapvoid.com.
17. Merriam-Webster. (n.d.). Definition of technology. *Merriam-Webster.com*. Retrieved from http://www.merriam-webster.com/dictionary/technology.

CHAPTER 2

1. Bostic, K. (2013, October 10). Apple's Jony Ive on design: "The most important thing is that you care". *Apple Insider*. Retrieved from http://appleinsider.com/articles/13/10/10/apples-jony-ive-on-design-the-most-important-thing-is-that-you-care.
2. Isaacson, W. (2011). Steve Jobs. New York: Simon & Schuster, pp. 6–45.
3. Adams, H. (2011, October 6). A tribute to a great artist: Steve Jobs. Smithsonian.com. Retrieved from http://www.smithsonianmag.com/arts-culture/A-Tribute-to-a-Great-Artist-Steve-Jobs.html.
4. Jobs, S. (2005, June 14). You've got to find what you love. *Stanford News*. Retrieved from http://news.stanford.edu/news/2005/june15/jobs-061505.html.
5. Rosoff, M. (2011, November 8). The music and books that inspired Steve Jobs. *Business Insider*. Retrieved from http://www.businessinsider.com/steve-jobs-music-books-2011-11?op=1.
6. Kahney, L. (2008). Inside Steve's Brain. New York: Penguin Group, p. 195.
7. Michalko, M. (2006). Thinkertoys. New York: Ten Speed Press.

8. Weintraub, S. (2012, March 2). Apple acknowledges use of Corning Gorilla Glass on iPhone, means Gorilla Glass 2 likely for iPhone 5. 9to5mac.com. Retrieved from http://9to5mac.com/2012/03/02/apple-acknowledges-use-of-corning-gorilla-glass-on-iphone-means-gorilla-glass-2-likely-for-iphone-5/.
9. I Sam. 17:40.
10. Segall, K. (2012). Insanely Simple. New York: Penguin Group, p. 139.
11. Kahney, L. (2008). Inside Steve's Brain. New York: Penguin Group, p. 86.
12. Kahney, L. (2008). Inside Steve's Brain. New York: Penguin Group, p. 51.
13. Kahney, L. (2008). Inside Steve's Brain. New York: Penguin Group, p. 96.
14. Segall, K. (2012). Insanely Simple. New York: Penguin Group, back cover.
15. Segall, K. (2012). Insanely Simple. New York: Penguin Group, p. 151.
16. Segall, K. (2012). Insanely Simple. New York: Penguin Group, front jacket.
17. Segall, K. (2012). Insanely Simple. New York: Penguin Group, pp. 1–10.
18. Brownlee, J. (2014, Nov. 18). Why Steve Jobs drowned the first iPod prototype. Cult of Mac. Retrieved from http://www.cultofmac.com/303469/steve-jobs-drowned-first-ipod-prototype/.
19. Segall, K. (2012). Insanely Simple. New York: Penguin Group, p. 163.
20. Isaacson, W. (2011). Steve Jobs. New York: Simon & Schuster, p. 349.
21. Brenner, J. (2016, April 1). On Apple's birthday, a look back at Steve Jobs and the "next" computer that could have been. *Newsweek*. Retrieved from http://www.newsweek.com/happy-40th-birthday-apple-443330.
22. Isaacson, W. (2011). Steve Jobs. New York: Simon & Schuster, p. 472.
23. Kahney, L. (2008). Inside Steve's Brain. New York: Penguin Group, p. 83.
24. Kahney, L. (2013). Jony Ive: The Genius Behind Apple's Greatest Products. New York: Portfolio/Penguin, p. 30.
25. Kahney, L. (2013). Jony Ive: The Genius Behind Apple's Greatest Products. New York: Portfolio/Penguin, pp. 28–29.
26. Kahney, L. (2013). Jony Ive: The Genius Behind Apple's Greatest Products. New York: Portfolio/Penguin, p. 29.
27. Isaacson, W. (2011). Steve Jobs. New York: Simon & Schuster, p. 342.
28. Brown, T. (2009). Change by Design. New York: Harper Business, p. 39.
29. Kahney, L. (2013). Jony Ive: The Genius Behind Apple's Greatest Products. New York: Portfolio/Penguin, p. 116.
30. Isaacson, W. (2011). Steve Jobs. New York: Simon & Schuster, p. 341.
31. Kahney, L. (2013). Jony Ive: The Genius Behind Apple's Greatest Products. New York: Portfolio/Penguin, pp. 22–23.
32. Kahney, L. (2013). Jony Ive: The Genius Behind Apple's Greatest Products. New York: Portfolio/Penguin, p. 190.
33. Kahney, L. (2013). Jony Ive: The Genius Behind Apple's Greatest Products. New York: Portfolio/Penguin, p. 269.

CHAPTER 3

1. Kahney, L. (2008). Inside Steve's Brain. New York: Penguin Group, p. 120.
2. Hackman, M.Z. and Johnson, C.E. (2009). Leadership—A Communication Perspective. Long Grove, IL: Waveland Press, Inc., p. 115.

3. Kouzes, J. and Posner, B. (2012). The Leadership Challenge: How to Make Extraordinary Things Happen in Organizations. San Francisco, CA: Jossey-Bass, p. 100.
4. Maxwell, J. (1993). Developing the Leader Within You. Nashville, TN: Thomas Nelson Publishers, pp. 139–140.
5. Kahney, L. (2009). Inside Steve's Brain. New York: Penguin Group, p. 278.
6. Isaacson, W. (2011). Steve Jobs. New York: Simon & Schuster, pp. 340–341.
7. Isaacson, W. (2011). Steve Jobs. New York: Simon & Schuster, p. 407.
8. Isaacson, W. (2011). Steve Jobs. New York: Simon & Schuster, p. 514.
9. Von, C. (2015). Apple employee welcome letter.
10. Isaacson, W. (2011). Steve Jobs. New York: Simon & Schuster, p. 567.
11. Kucera, D. and Nazareth, R. (2011, August 26). Apple without CEO Jobs gives Cook $28 billion to deal: Real M&A. Bloomberg. Retrieved from http://www.bloomberg.com/news/2011-08-26/apple-without-jobs-as-ceo-gives-cook-28-billion-to-make-a-deal-real-m-a.html.
12. Brian, M. (2011, August 25). A look at Apple's CEOs from 1977 to 2011. The Next Web. Retrieved from http://thenextweb.com/apple/2011/08/25/a-look-at-apples-ceos-from-1977-to-2011/.
13. Feloni, R. (2014, February 25). Food network Chef Robert Irvine shares the top 5 reasons restaurants fail. Business Insider. Retrieved from http://www.businessinsider.com/why-restaurants-fail-so-often-2014-2.
14. Union Square Hospitality Group. (2016). Company News. www.ushgnyc.com/company (accessed February 4, 2017).
15. Meyer, D. (2008). Setting the Table. New York: Harper, p. 2.
16. Meyer, D. (2008). Setting the Table. New York: Harper, p. 4.
17. Meyer, D. (2008). Setting the Table. New York: Harper, p. 20.
18. Meyer, D. (2008). Setting the Table. New York: Harper, p. 189.

CHAPTER 4

1. Gladwell, M. (2008). Outliers. New York: Little Brown and Company.
2. Boyle, D., Casaday, G., Colson, C., Gordon, M., Rudin (Producer), S., and Boyle (Director), D. (2015). Steve Jobs [Motion Picture]. Universal City, CA: Universal Pictures.
3. Isaacson, W. (2011). Steve Jobs. New York: Simon & Schuster, p. 118.
4. Isaacson, W. (2011). Steve Jobs. New York: Simon & Schuster, p. 119.
5. Northouse, P.G. (2013). Leadership. Thousand Oaks, CA: Sage, pp. 23–26.
6. Northouse, P.G. (2013). Leadership. Thousand Oaks, CA: Sage, pp. 44–46.
7. Kamprad, I. (1976). Testament of a Furniture Dealer, p. 2. Retrieved July 16, 2016, from http://www.ikea.com/ms/en_US/pdf/reports-downloads/the-testament-of-a-furniture-dealer.pdf.
8. Bartlett, C.A. and Nanda, A. (1996). Ingvar Kamprad and IKEA, p. 3. Retrieved July 18, 2016, from http://www.hbs.edu/faculty/Pages/item.aspx?num=11717.
9. Bartlett, C.A. and Nanda, A. (1996). Ingvar Kamprad and IKEA, p. 1. Retrieved July 18, 2016, from http://www.hbs.edu/faculty/Pages/item.aspx?num=11717.
10. Bartlett, C.A. and Nanda, A. (1996). Ingvar Kamprad and IKEA, p. 2. Retrieved July 18, 2016, from http://www.hbs.edu/faculty/Pages/item.aspx?num=11717.

11. Bartlett, C.A. and Nanda, A. (1996). *Ingvar Kamprad and IKEA*, pp. 5, 8. Retrieved July 18, 2016, from http://www.hbs.edu/faculty/Pages/item.aspx?num=11717.
12. Kamprad, I. (1976). *Testament of a Furniture Dealer*, p. 3. Retrieved July 16, 2016, from http://www.ikea.com/ms/en_US/pdf/reports-downloads/the-testament-of-a-furniture-dealer.pdf.
13. Carmichael, E. (2011, January 24). Ingvar Kamprad documentary—Success story. *YouTube*. Retrieved from https://www.youtube.com/watch?v=fhQt08zBVzw.

CHAPTER 5

1. 2 Sam. 23:8–39; I Chr. 11–12.
2. Schlender, B. and Tetzeli, R. (2015). Becoming Steve Jobs. New York: Crown Business, p. 14.
3. Schlender, B. and Tetzeli, R. (2015). Becoming Steve Jobs. New York: Crown Business, pp. 28–29.
4. Isaacson, W. (2011). Steve Jobs. New York: Simon & Schuster, p. 84.
5. Isaacson, W. (2011). Steve Jobs. New York: Simon & Schuster, pp. 363, 115.
6. Isaacson, W. (2011). Steve Jobs. New York: Simon & Schuster, p. 64.
7. DiStefano, P. (2016, February). From the Chancellor. University of Colorado Boulder. Retrieved from http://www.colorado.edu/chancellor/2016/02/24/chancellor.
8. Isaacson, W. (2011). Steve Jobs. New York: Simon & Schuster, p. 62.
9. Isaacson, W. (2011). Steve Jobs. New York: Simon & Schuster, p. 61.
10. Isaacson, W. (2011). Steve Jobs. New York: Simon & Schuster, p. 144.
11. Schlender, B. and Tetzeli, R. (2015). Becoming Steve Jobs. New York: Crown Business, p. 60.
12. Isaacson, W. (2011). Steve Jobs. New York: Simon & Schuster, pp. 102–104.
13. Isaacson, W. (2011). Steve Jobs. New York: Simon & Schuster, pp. 110–112.
14. Isaacson, W. (2011). Steve Jobs. New York: Simon & Schuster, p. 113.
15. Isaacson, W. (2011). Steve Jobs. New York: Simon & Schuster, pp. 115, 192.
16. Isaacson, W. (2011). Steve Jobs. New York: Simon & Schuster, p. 142.
17. Isaacson, W. (2011). Steve Jobs. New York: Simon & Schuster, p. 114.
18. Kahney, L. (2009). Inside Steve's Brain. New York: Penguin Group, p. 106.
19. Isaacson, W. (2011). Steve Jobs. New York: Simon & Schuster, pp. 110, 143–144.
20. Hastings, R. (2009, August 1). Netflix Culture: Freedom & Responsibility. *Slideshare. net*. Retrieved from http://www.slideshare.net/reed2001/culture-1798664.
21. Isaacson, W. (2011). Steve Jobs. New York: Simon & Schuster, p. 185.
22. Schlender, B. and Tetzeli, R. (2015). Becoming Steve Jobs. New York: Crown Business, pp. 319–320.
23. Isaacson, W. (2011). Steve Jobs. New York: Simon & Schuster, p. 460.
24. Frommer, D. (2016, Oct. 5). Watch some of Steve Jobs's best interviews, five years after his death. *Recode*. Retrieved from http://www.recode.net/2016/10/5/13171430/steve-jobs-apple-conference-swisher-mossberg.
25. Segall, K. (2012). Insanely Simple. New York: Penguin Group, p. 32.
26. Segall, K. (2012). Insanely Simple. New York: Penguin Group, p. 44.
27. Lashinsky, A. (2012). Inside Apple: How America's Most Admired—and Secretive—Company Really Works. New York: Business Plus, p. 81.

28. Segall, K. (2012). Insanely Simple. New York: Penguin Group, p. 27.
29. Segall, K. (2012). Insanely Simple. New York: Penguin Group, p. 26.
30. Golf Staff Writers (2010). In his new book, Paul Azinger reveals the key pieces of his strategy that helped the U.S. team capture the Ryder Cup. Golf. Retrieved from http://www.golf.com/tour-and-news/his-new-book-paul-azinger-reveals-key-pieces-his-strategy-helped-us-team-capture-ryder.
31. Yang, J.L. (2006, June 1). The Power of 4.6. *Fortune CNN Money.* Retrieved from http://money.cnn.com/popups/2006/fortune/greatteams_teamonomics/frameset.10.exclude.html.
32. Bennett, D. (2016, June 17). Nike's Phil Knight on selling personality and performance. *Marketing.* Retrieved from http://www.marketingmag.ca/brands/nikes-phil-knight-on-selling-personality-and-performance-176848.
33. Friedman, V. (2015, May 29). Nike is the most valuable apparel brand in the World. *New York Times.* Retrieved from http://www.nytimes.com/2015/05/30/fashion/nike-is-the-most-valuable-apparel-brand-in-the-world.html?_r=1.
34. Gould, S. and Lutz, A. (2015, May 22). See how Nike dominates the shoe industry in one chart. *Business Insider.* Retrieved from http://www.businessinsider.com/see-how-nike-dominates-the-shoe-industry-in-one-chart-2015-5.
35. Soni, P. (2014, December 29). Market share gain spurs NIKE's North American footwear revenues. *Market Realist.* Retrieved from http://marketrealist.com/2014/12/market-share-gain-spurs-nikes-north-american-footwear-revenues/.
36. Martin, E. (2015, August 23). How Phil Knight built Nike into one of the biggest brands in the world and became a billionaire. *Business Insider.* Retrieved from http://www.businessinsider.com/nike-founder-phil-knight-profile-2015-8/#phil-knight-was-born-on-february-24-1938-he-ran-track-at-the-university-of-oregon-and-graduated-in-1959-with-a-degree-in-journalism-after-serving-in-the-army-for-a-year-he-went-back-to-school-to-earn-his-mba-from-stanfords-graduate-school-of-business-1.
37. Knight, P. (2016). Shoe Dog: A Memoir by the Creator of Nike (Kindle Location 47). Scribner. Kindle Edition.
38. Knight, P. (2016). Shoe Dog: A Memoir by the Creator of Nike (Kindle Locations 274–277). Scribner. Kindle Edition.
39. Knight, P. (2016). Shoe Dog: A Memoir by the Creator of Nike (Kindle Locations 220–225). Scribner. Kindle Edition.
40. Knight, P. (2016). Shoe Dog: A Memoir by the Creator of Nike (Kindle Locations 225–229). Scribner. Kindle Edition.
41. Knight, P. (2016). Shoe Dog: A Memoir by the Creator of Nike (Kindle Locations 225–232). Scribner. Kindle Edition.
42. Knight, P. (2016). Shoe Dog: A Memoir by the Creator of Nike (Kindle Locations 54–56). Scribner. Kindle Edition.
43. Knight, P. (2016). Shoe Dog: A Memoir by the Creator of Nike (Kindle Locations 17–22). Scribner. Kindle Edition.
44. Knight, P. (2016). Shoe Dog: A Memoir by the Creator of Nike (Kindle Locations 77). Scribner. Kindle Edition.
45. Knight, P. (2016). Shoe Dog: A Memoir by the Creator of Nike (Kindle Locations 56–61). Scribner. Kindle Edition.
46. Knight, P. (2016). Shoe Dog: A Memoir by the Creator of Nike (Kindle Locations 98–102). Scribner. Kindle Edition.
47. Knight, P. (2016). Shoe Dog: A Memoir by the Creator of Nike (Kindle Locations 393–399). Scribner. Kindle Edition.

48. Knight, P. (2016). Shoe Dog: A Memoir by the Creator of Nike (Kindle Locations 721). Scribner. Kindle Edition.
49. Rose, C. (2016, April 28). Phil Knight. *Charlie Rose*. Retrieved from https://charlierose.com/videos/28031.
50. Knight, P. (2016). Shoe Dog: A Memoir by the Creator of Nike (Kindle Locations 4189–4193). Scribner. Kindle Edition.
51. McCue, M. (2013, Feb. 26). Employee Number One. *Runner's World*. Retrieved from http://www.runnersworld.com/masters/employee-number-one.
52. Rovell, D. (2016, April 26). Nike founder Phil Knight's new book reveals remarkable history. *ESPN*. Retrieved from http://www.espn.com/espn/story/_/id/15385868/nike-founder-phil-knight-new-book-reveals-remarkable-history.
53. Knight, P. (2016). Shoe Dog: A Memoir by the Creator of Nike (Kindle Locations 1161). Scribner. Kindle Edition.
54. Knight, P. (2016). Shoe Dog: A Memoir by the Creator of Nike (Kindle Locations 3289–3290, 4549). Scribner. Kindle Edition.
55. Wolman, D. (2016, June 13). Meet the man who reinvented Nike, Seduced Adidas, and helped make Portland the sports gear capital of the World. *Portland Monthly*. Retrieved from http://www.pdxmonthly.com/articles/2016/6/13/meet-the-man-who-reinvented-nike-seduced-adidas-and-helped-make-portland-the-sports-gear-capital-of-the-world.
56. Knight, P. (2016). Shoe Dog: A Memoir by the Creator of Nike (Kindle Locations 3274–3275). Scribner. Kindle Edition.
57. Knight, P. (2016). Shoe Dog: A Memoir by the Creator of Nike (Kindle Locations 4222-4225). Scribner. Kindle Edition.
58. Knight, P. (2016). Shoe Dog: A Memoir by the Creator of Nike (Kindle Locations 4196-4203). Scribner. Kindle Edition.
59. Scribner (2016, Apr 26). Shoe Dog: Press Release. *Simon & Schuster Digital Catalog*. Retrieved from https://catalog.simonandschuster.com/TitleDetails/TitleDetails.aspx?cid=12939&pn=1&isbn=9781501150111&FilterBy=21&FilterVal=Biography+%26+Autobiography&FilterByName=Category&ob=0&ed=&showcart=N&camefrom=&find=&a=.

CHAPTER 6

1. McLeod, H. (2013, July 18). Culture is the #1 metric. *Gaping Void*. Retrieved from https://www.gapingvoid.com/blog/2013/07/18/culture1/.
2. Burke, W.W. (2014). Organization Change: Theory and Practice. Thousand Oaks, CA: Sage Publications, Inc., p. 22.
3. Parr, S. (2012, January 24). Culture eats strategy for lunch. *Fast Company*. Retrieved from http://www.fastcompany.com/1810674/culture-eats-strategy-lunch.
4. Deal, T.E. and Kennedy, A.A. (1982). Corporate Culture: Rites and Rituals of Corporate Life. Reading, MA: Addison-Wesley.
5. Frommer, D. (2009, November 12). It's harder to get a job at the apple store than it is to get into Harvard. *Business Insider*. Retrieved from http://www.businessinsider.com/its-harder-to-get-a-job-at-the-apple-store-than-it-is-to-get-into-harvard-2009-11.
6. Schein, E. (2010). Organizational Culture and Leadership, 4th edn. San Francisco, CA: Jossey-Bass.

7. Sloan, P. (2012, September 12). Apple by the numbers: 84M iPads, 400M iOS devices, 350M iPods sold. *Cnet*. Retrieved from https://www.cnet.com/news/apple-by-the-numbers-84m-ipads-400m-ios-devices-350m-ipods-sold/.

8. Costello, S. (2017, March 21). This is the number of iPods sold all-time. *Lifewire*. Retrieved from https://www.lifewire.com/number-of-ipods-sold-all-time-1999515.

9. France-Presse, A. (2014, February 26). Nokia, BlackBerry and Motorola in search of lost glory. *Gadgets 360*. Retrieved from http://gadgets.ndtv.com/mobiles/news/nokia-blackberry-and-motorola-in-search-of-lost-glory-488718.

10. Apple (2016, July 27). Apple celebrates one billion iPhones. *Apple*. Retrieved from http://www.apple.com/newsroom/2016/07/apple-celebrates-one-billion-iphones.html.

11. Zipkin, N. (2014, October 13). Finland blames Apple for economic problems. *Entrepreneur*. Retrieved from https://www.entrepreneur.com/article/238431.

12. La Monica, P.R. (2016, September 28). End of an era: BlackBerry will stop making its own phones. *CNN Tech*. Retrieved from https://money.cnn.com/2016/09/28/technology/blackberry-outsource-phones/.

13. Isaacson, W. (2011). Steve Jobs. New York: Simon & Schuster, p. 369.

14. Isaacson, W. (2011). Steve Jobs. New York: Simon & Schuster, p. 370.

15. Isaacson, W. (2011). Steve Jobs. New York: Simon & Schuster, p. 375.

16. Wahba, P. (2015, March 13). Apple extends lead in U.S. top 10 retailers by sales per square foot. *Fortune*. Retrieved from http://fortune.com/2015/03/13/apples-holiday-top-10-retailers-iphone/.

17. Isaacson, W. (2011). Steve Jobs. New York: Simon & Schuster, p. 165.

18. Kahney, L. (2008). Inside Steve's Brain. New York: Penguin Group, pp. 87–89.

19. Isaacson, W. (2011). Steve Jobs. New York: Simon & Schuster, pp. 123–124.

20. Isaacson, W. (2011). Steve Jobs. New York: Simon & Schuster, p. 83.

21. Chapman, G.D. (2014). The 5 Love Languages: The Secret to Love That Lasts. Chicago, IL: Northfield Publishing.

22. Scott, F. (2016, May 28). Is this the greatest graduation speech ever? *MailOnline*. Retrieved from http://www.dailymail.co.uk/news/article-3613934/Donovan-Livingston-s-Harvard-graduation-speech-inspires-America-world-including-Hillary-Clinton-Justin-Timberlake.html.

23. Livingston, D. (2016, May 25). LIft Off. *Harvard Graduate School of Education*. Retrieved from http://www.gse.harvard.edu/news/16/05/lift.

24. Zappos (n.d.). The Zappos family story: In the beginning—Let there be shoes. *Zappos*. Retrieved from http://www.zappos.com/c/about-zappos.

25. Krishnan, S. (2012, January 11). The legend of Zappos—Building a brand with great customer service. *Freshdesk*. Retrieved from http://blog.freshdesk.com/the-legend-of-zappos-building-a-brand-with-gr/.

26. Bloomberg (2010, May 27). Tony Hsieh: Redefining Zappos' business model. *Bloomberg*. Retrieved from http://www.bloomberg.com/news/articles/2010-05-27/tony-hsieh-redefining-zappos-business-model.

27. Mitchell, D. (2008, May 24). Shoe seller's secret of success. *New York Times*. Retrieved from http://www.nytimes.com/2008/05/24/technology/24online.html.

28. Edwards, J. (2012, January 9). Check out the insane lengths Zappos customer service reps will go to. *Business Insider*. Retrieved from http://www.businessinsider.com/zappos-customer-service-crm-2012-1.

29. Working, R. (2013, August 22). 8 ridiculous ways Zappos keeps customers and staffers happy. *Ragan*. Retrieved from http://www.ragan.com/Main/Articles/8_ridiculous_ways_Zappos_keeps_customers_and_staff_47186.aspx.

30. Hsieh, T. (2006, September 1). How I did it: Tony Hsieh, CEO, Zappos.com. *Inc*. Retrieved from http://www.inc.com/magazine/20060901/hidi-hsieh.html.

31. Fass, A. (2012, November 15). Tony Hsieh: "I Fire Those Who Don't Fit Our Company Culture". *Inc*. Retrieved from http://www.inc.com/allison-fass/tony-hsieh-zappos-i-fire-non-culture-fits-fast.html.

32. Nisen, M. (2013, November 22). Tony Hsieh's brilliant strategy for hiring kind people. *Business Insider*. Retrieved from http://www.businessinsider.com/tony-hsieh-zappos-hiring-strategy-2013-11.

33. Reh, F.J. (2014). Culture is a firing offense. *About.com*. Retrieved from http://management.about.com/od/organizationaldev/a/Culture-Is-A-Firing-Offense.htm.

34. Zappos. (n.d.). How much could happiness save you? *Zappos*. Retrieved from http://deliveringhappiness.com/services/.

CHAPTER 7

1. MacDailyNews. (2016, May 16). When Steve Jobs told Larry Ellison how he'd save Apple. *MacDailyNews*. Retrieved from http://macdailynews.com/2016/05/16/when-steve-jobs-told-larry-ellison-how-hed-save-apple/.

2. Gandel, S. (2016, February 2). World's most valuable company. *Fortune*. Retrieved from http://fortune.com/2016/02/02/apple-google-alphabet-2/.

3. Badenhausen, K. (2016, May 31). Apple, Google top the world's most valuable brands of 2016. *Forbes*. Retrieved from http://www.forbes.com/sites/kurtbadenhausen/2016/05/11/the-worlds-most-valuable-brands/#442c50367561.

4. Rogers, A. (2016, February 19). Customer loyalty and retention: Key driver for Apple. *Market Realist*. Retrieved from http://marketrealist.com/2016/02/customer-loyalty-retention-key-driver-apple/.

5. Ballard, B. (2014, November 3). Apple has brand loyalty that most companies can only dream of. *Betanews*. Retrieved from http://betanews.com/2015/04/09/apple-has-brand-loyalty-that-most-companies-can-only-dream-of/.

6. Richter, R. (2014, July 15). Apple Beats Competitors In Smartphone Brand Loyalty. *Statista*. Retrieved from https://www.statista.com/chart/2460/brand-retention-in-the-smartphone-industry/.

7. Deidu, H. (2015, December 6). Apple success all about customer loyalty: Deidu. *Bloomberg*. Retrieved from http://www.bloomberg.com/news/videos/b/e20f3c00-605f-4054-8bde-1047440eefc5.

8. Carson, B. (2015, October 22). Steve Jobs' reaction to this insult shows why he was such a great CEO. *Yahoo Finance*. Retrieved from http://finance.yahoo.com/news/steve-jobs-reaction-insult-shows-232452854.html.

9. Isaacson, W. (2011). Steve Jobs. New York: Simon & Schuster, p. 95.

10. Isaacson, W. (2011). Steve Jobs. New York: Simon & Schuster, p. 97.

11. Isaacson, W. (2011). Steve Jobs. New York: Simon & Schuster, p. 98.

12. Tweedie, S. (2016, April 16). 21 tiny design features that show Apple's incredible attention to detail. *Business Insider*. Retrieved from http://www.businessinsider.com/best-apple-design-details?utm_source=loopinsight.com&utm_medium=referral&utm_campaign=Feed%3A+loopinsight%2FKqJb+(The+Loop)&utm_content=FeedBurner.

13. Prigg, M. (2015, March 20). Apple reveals the secret fitness lab it has been using for two years to develop its health tracking watch. *MailOnline*. Retrieved from http://www.dailymail.co.uk/sciencetech/article-3004701/Apple-reveals-secret-fitness-lab-using-TWO-YEARS-develop-movement-tracking-watch.html.

14. Welsh, C. (2015, December 20). The iPhone's camera is so good because 800 people are working on it. *The Verge*. Retrieved from http://www.theverge.com/2015/12/20/10631330/iphone-camera-team-800-people.

15. Apple. (n.d.). Apple watch—Series 2. *Apple*. Retrieved from http://www.apple.com/apple-watch-series-2/.

16. Brown, T. (2009). Change by Design. New York: Harper Business, p. 49.

17. Isaacson, W. (2011). Steve Jobs. New York: Simon & Schuster, p. 407.

18. Brown, T. (2009). Change by Design. New York: Harper Business, pp. 13–15.

19. Brown, T. and Wyatt, J. (2010, Winter). Design thinking for social innovation. *Stanford Social Innovation Review*. Retrieved from https://ssir.org/articles/entry/design_thinking_for_social_innovation.

20. Pastorek, W. (2013, November 12). Bringing design thinking to social problems, Ideo.org focuses on the people in need. *Co.exist*. Retrieved from https://www.fastcoexist.com/3020789/change-generation/bringing-design-thinking-to-social-problems-ideoorg-focuses-on-the-people.

21. Peters, T. and Waterman, R.H. (2004). In Search of Excellence. New York: HarperCollins Publishers.

22. Collins, J.C. and Porras, J.I. (2011). Built to Last: Successful Habits of Visionary Companies. New York: HarperCollins.

23. 3M. (2015). 3M Performance. *3M.com*. Retrieved from http://solutions.3m.com/wps/portal/3M/en_US/3M-Company/Information/Profile/Performance/.

24. 3M. (2015). 3M Awards. *3M.com*. Retrieved from http://solutions.3m.com/wps/portal/3M/en_US/3M-Company/Information/Profile/Performance/.

25. Kalb, I. (2013, July 8). Innovation isn't just about brainstorming new ideas. *Business Insider*. Retrieved from http://www.businessinsider.com/innovate-or-die-a-mantra-for-every-business2013-7.

26. Winton, A. (2012, May 15). 3M's sustainability innovation machine. *Harvard Business Review*. Retrieved from https://hbr.org/2012/05/3ms-sustainability-innovation.

27. von Hippel, E., Thomke, S., and Sonnack, M. (1999, September–October). Creating breakthroughs at 3M. *Harvard Business Review*. Retrieved from https://hbr.org/1999/09/creating-breakthroughs-at-3m.

28. 3M. (2016). 3M History. *3M.com*. Retrieved from http://solutions.3m.com/wps/portal/3M/en_US/3M-Company/Information/Profile/Performance/.

29. Govindarajan, V. and Srinivas, S. (2013, August 6). The innovation mindset in action: 3M corporation. *Harvard Business Review*. Retrieved from https://hbr.org/2013/08/the-innovation-mindset-in-acti-3.

30. Lukas, P. (2003, April 1). 3M a mining company built on a mistake stuck it out until a young man came along with ideas about how to tape those blunders together as innovations—Leading to decades of growth. *CNNMoney*. Retrieved from http://money.cnn.com/magazines/fsb/fsb_archive/2003/04/01/341016/.

31. Kelley, T. and Kelley, D. (2013). Creative Confidence. New York: Crown Business.

32. Goetz, K. (2011, February 1). How 3M gave everyone days off and created an innovation dynamo. *Fast Company*. Retrieved from http://www.fastcodesign.com/1663137/how-3m-gave-everyone-days-off-and-created-an-innovation-dynamo.

33. Vonn, S.R. (2011, August 18). Post-it notes are one of the few office supplies that really innovated. *Zuma Office*. Retrieved from http://officesuppliesblog.zumaoffice.com/office-supplies-shopping-tips/post-it-notes-are-one-of-the-few-office-supplies-that-really-innovated/.

34. Sharma, A. (2013, June 26). The 3M you don't know. *The Motley Fool*. Retrieved from http://www.fool.com/investing/general/2013/06/26/the-3m-you-dont-know.aspx.

35. Colvin, G. (2013, February 28). Built for brilliance. *Fortune*. Retrieved from http://fortune.com/2013/02/28/the-worlds-most-admired-companies-built-for-brilliance/.

36. Kelley, T. and Kelley, D. (2013). Creative Confidence. New York: Crown Business, Front flap.

CHAPTER 8

1. Isaacson, W. (2011). Steve Jobs. New York: Simon & Schuster, p. 143.

2. Ringel, M., Taylor, A., and Zablit, H. (2015). *The Most Innovative Companies 2015*. Retrieved July 25, 2016, from https://media-publications.bcg.com/MIC/BCG-Most-Innovative-Companies-2015-Nov-2015.pdf.

3. Kahney, L. (2008). Inside Steve's Brain. New York: Penguin Group, p. 179.

4. Welsh, J. (2005). Winning. New York: Harper Business.

5. Bossidy, L. and Charan, R. (2002). Execution: The Discipline of Getting Things Done. New York: Crown Business.

6. Bossidy, L. and Charan, R. (2002). Execution: The Discipline of Getting Things Done. New York: Crown Business, front inside page.

7. Kahney, L. (2008). Inside Steve's Brain. New York: Penguin Group, p. 182.

8. Segall, K. (2012). Insanely Simple. New York: Penguin Group, p. 50.

9. Segall, K. (2012). Insanely Simple. New York: Penguin Group, p. 72.

10. Isaacson, W. (2011). Steve Jobs. New York: Simon & Schuster, p. 570.

11. Segall, K. (2012). Insanely Simple. New York: Penguin Group, pp. 34–35.

12. Lashinsky, A. (2012). Inside Apple: How America's Most Admired—and Secretive—Company Really Works. New York: Business Plus, p. 67.

13. Lashinsky, A. (2012). Inside Apple: How America's Most Admired—and Secretive—Company Really Works. New York: Business Plus, pp. 67–68.

14. Isaacson, W. (2011). Steve Jobs. New York: Simon & Schuster, p. 161.

15. Isaacson, W. (2011). Steve Jobs. New York: Simon & Schuster, p. 170.

16. Statista. (2016). Statistics and facts on Starbucks. *Statista*. Retrieved from https://www.statista.com/topics/1246/Starbucks/.

17. Statista. (2015). Leading coffee house chains ranked by number of stores worldwide in 2015. *Statista*. Retrieved from https://www.statista.com/statistics/272900/coffee-house-chains-ranked-by-number-of-stores-worldwide/.

18. Swift, C. (2013, October 23). Did you know? the top ten most traded commodities. *Rogers Family Coffee*. Retrieved from http://www.rogersfamilyco.com/index.php/know-top-ten-traded-commodities/.

19. Goldschein, E. (2011, November 14). 11 incredible facts about the global coffee industry. *Business Insider*. Retrieved from http://www.businessinsider.com/facts-about-the-coffee-industry-2011-11.

20. Schultz, H. and Yang, D.J. (1997). Pour Your Heart Into It. New York: Hachette Books, p. 76.

21. Schultz, H. and Yang, D.J. (1997). Pour Your Heart Into It. New York: Hachette Books, p. 51.

22. Schultz, H. and Yang, D.J. (1997). Pour Your Heart Into It. New York: Hachette Books, p. 50.

23. Schultz, H. and Yang, D.J. (1997). Pour Your Heart Into It. New York: Hachette Books, pp. 52–53.

24. Schultz, H. and Yang, D.J. (1997). Pour Your Heart Into It. New York: Hachette Books, p. 19.

25. Schultz, H. and Yang, D.J. (1997). Pour Your Heart Into It. New York: Hachette Books, p. 55.

26. Schultz, H. and Yang, D.J. (1997). Pour Your Heart Into It. New York: Hachette Books, pp. 59–60.

27. Schultz, H. and Yang, D.J. (1997). Pour Your Heart Into It. New York: Hachette Books, pp. 58–60.

28. Schultz, H. and Yang, D.J. (1997). Pour Your Heart Into It. New York: Hachette Books, pp. 61–62.

29. Schultz, H. and Yang, D.J. (1997). Pour Your Heart Into It. New York: Hachette Books, p. 62.

30. Schultz, H. and Yang, D.J. (1997). Pour Your Heart Into It. New York: Hachette Books, p. 61.

31. Schultz, H. and Yang, D.J. (1997). Pour Your Heart Into It. New York: Hachette Books, p. 66.

32. Schultz, H. and Yang, D.J. (1997). Pour Your Heart Into It. New York: Hachette Books, pp. 68–69.

33. Schultz, H. and Yang, D.J. (1997). Pour Your Heart Into It. New York: Hachette Books, p. 67.

34. Schultz, H. and Yang, D.J. (1997). Pour Your Heart Into It. New York: Hachette Books, p. 90.

35. Schultz, H. and Yang, D.J. (1997). Pour Your Heart Into It. New York: Hachette Books, pp. 92–93.

36. Schultz, H. and Yang, D.J. (1997). Pour Your Heart Into It. New York: Hachette Books, pp. 93.

37. Schultz, H. and Yang, D.J. (1997). Pour Your Heart Into It. New York: Hachette Books, pp. 93–94.

38. Craft Beverage Jobs. (2016, April 17). The history of first, second, and third wave coffee. *Craft Beverage Jobs*. Retrieved from https://www.craftbeveragejobs.com/the-history-of-first-second-and-third-wave-coffee-22315/.

39. Schultz, H. and Yang, D.J. (1997). Pour Your Heart Into It. New York: Hachette Books, p. 5.

40. Schultz, H. and Yang, D.J. (1997). Pour Your Heart Into It. New York: Hachette Books, p. 119.

CHAPTER 9

1. Isaacson, W. (2011). Steve Jobs. New York, NY: Simon & Schuster, p. 488.

2. Lashinsky, A. (2012). Inside Apple: How America"s Most Admired—and Secretive—Company Really Works. New York: Business Plus, p. 59.

3. Lashinsky, A. (2012). Inside Apple: How America's Most Admired—and Secretive—Company Really Works. New York: Business Plus, p. 58–59.

4. Isaacson, W. (2011). Steve Jobs. New York: Simon & Schuster, p. 359.

5. Lashinsky, A. (2012). Inside Apple: How America's Most Admired—and Secretive—Company Really Works. New York: Business Plus, p. 60.

6. Lashinsky, A. (2012). Inside Apple: How America's Most Admired—and Secretive—Company Really Works. New York: Business Plus, pp. 62–63.

7. Kahney, L. (2008). Inside Steve's Brain. New York: Penguin Group, pp. 41–42.

8. Lashinsky, A. (2012). Inside Apple: How America's Most Admired—and Secretive—Company Really Works. New York: Business Plus, p. 61.

9. Kahney, L. (2008). Inside Steve's Brain. New York: Penguin Group, p. 30.

10. Lashinsky, A. (2012). Inside Apple: How America's Most Admired—and Secretive—Company Really Works. New York: Business Plus, p. 63.

11. Kim, W.C. and Mauborgne, R. (2014, May). Blue ocean leadership. *Harvard Business Review, 92*, 65.

12. Isaacson, W. (2011). Steve Jobs. New York: Simon & Schuster, p. 94.

13. Segall, K. (2012). Insanely Simple. New York: Penguin Group, p. 6.

14. Segall, K. (2012). Insanely Simple. New York: Penguin Group, pp. 90–91.

15. Apple (n.d.). Apple watch edition. *Apple*. Retrieved from http://www.apple.com/apple-watch-edition/.

16. Kuhlmann, A. and Philp, B. (2009). The Orange Code: How ING Direct Succeeded by Being a Rebel with a Cause. Hoboken, NJ: John Wiley & Sons, Inc., p. 36.

17. Kuhlmann, A. and Philp, B. (2009). The Orange Code: How ING Direct Succeeded by Being a Rebel with a Cause. Hoboken, NJ: John Wiley & Sons, Inc., p. xv.

18. Kuhlmann, A. and Philp, B. (2009). The Orange Code: How ING Direct Succeeded by Being a Rebel with a Cause. Hoboken, NJ: John Wiley & Sons, Inc., p. xvi.

19. De La Merced, M.J. (2011). Capital one to buy ING's online bank for $9 billion. *The New York Times*. Retrieved from http://dealbook.nytimes.com/2011/06/16/capital-one-to-buy-ings-u-s-online-banking-unit-for-9-billion/?_r=0 (accessed November 20, 2013).

20. Forbes, S. (2011), Steve Forbes interview: How ING Direct's Arkadi Kuhlmann became the 'CEO Of Savings'. *Forbes*, p. 2. Retrieved from http://www.forbes.com/sites/steveforbes/2011/05/09/arkadi-kuhlmann-transcript/3/ (accessed November 20, 2013).

21. Time Staff. (2007). ING Direct's man on a mission. *Time*. Retrieved from http://content.time.com/time/subscriber/article/0,33009,1633064-1,00.html (accessed November 25, 2013).

22. Dummett, B. (2013). 'Canada's big five banks didn't disappoint, reporting strong earnings across the board. *The Wall Street Journal*. Retrieved from http://blogs.wsj.com/canadarealtime/2013/08/29/canadas-big-five-banks-didnt-disappoint-reporting-strong-earnings-across-the-board/ (accessed November 25, 2013).

23. Kuhlmann, A. and Philp, B. (2009). The Orange Code: How ING Direct Succeeded by Being a Rebel with a Cause. Hoboken, NJ: John Wiley & Sons, Inc., pp. 6–7,13–14.

24. Forbes, S. (2011, May 9). Steve Forbes interview: How ING direct's Arkadi Kuhlmann became the "CEO of savings". *Forbes*. Retrieved from https://www.forbes.com/sites/steveforbes/2011/05/09/arkadi-kuhlmann-transcript/#27e07e18a733.

25. Mathew, J., Gopakumar, M.K.T., Karattuchali, N.P., and Gangadharan, S. (2008). ING case study. *Liverpool Business School*, p. 3. Retrieved from http://www.slideshare.net/sreeragtg/ing-final-report (accessed November 18, 2013).

26. Kuhlmann, A. and Philp, B. (2009). The Orange Code: How ING Direct Succeeded by Being a Rebel with a Cause. Hoboken, NJ: John Wiley & Sons, Inc., p. 16.

27. Kuhlmann, A. and Philp, B. (2009). The Orange Code: How ING Direct Succeeded by Being a Rebel with a Cause. Hoboken, NJ: John Wiley & Sons, Inc., p. 17.
28. Time Staff (2007). ING direct's man on a mission. *Time*, p. 2. Retrieved from http://content.time.com/time/subscriber/article/0,33009,1633064-1,00.html (accessed November 25, 2013).
29. Greenberg, K. 2010. ING CEO on customers: More dating, less marriage. *Media Post*. Retrieved from http://www.mediapost.com/publications/article/139308/ (accessed November 26, 2013).
30. Forbes, S. (2011). Steve Forbes interview: How ING direct's Arkadi Kuhlmann became the 'CEO Of Savings'. *Forbes*, p. 3. Retrieved from http://www.forbes.com/sites/steve-forbes/2011/05/09/arkadi-kuhlmann-transcript/3/ (accessed November 20, 2013).
31. Kuhlmann, A. and Philp, B. (2009). The Orange Code: How ING Direct Succeeded by Being a Rebel with a Cause. Hoboken, NJ: John Wiley & Sons, Inc., p. 42.
32. Kuhlmann, A. and Philp, B. (2009). The Orange Code: How ING Direct Succeeded by Being a Rebel with a Cause. Hoboken, NJ: John Wiley & Sons, Inc., pp. 17, 83, 85.
33. Mathew, J., Gopakumar, M.K.T., Karattuchali, N.P., and Gangadharan, S. (2008), ING case study. *Liverpool Business School*, p. 3. Retrieved from http://www.slideshare.net/sreeragtg/ing-final-report (accessed November 18, 2013), appendix 6.
34. Kuhlmann, A. and Philp, B. (2009). The Orange Code: How ING Direct Succeeded by Being a Rebel with a Cause. Hoboken, NJ: John Wiley & Sons, Inc., p. 106.
35. Kuhlmann, A. and Philp, B. (2009). The Orange Code: How ING Direct Succeeded by Being a Rebel with a Cause. Hoboken, NJ: John Wiley & Sons, Inc., p. 107.
36. Kuhlmann, A. and Philp, B. (2009). The Orange Code: How ING Direct Succeeded by Being a Rebel with a Cause. Hoboken, NJ: John Wiley & Sons, Inc., p. 18.
37. Kuhlmann, A. and Philp, B. (2009). The Orange Code: How ING Direct Succeeded by Being a Rebel with a Cause. Hoboken, NJ: John Wiley & Sons, Inc., p. 116.
38. Kuhlmann, A. and Philp, B. (2009). The Orange Code: How ING Direct Succeeded by Being a Rebel with a Cause. Hoboken, NJ: John Wiley & Sons, Inc., p. 97.

CHAPTER 10

1. Schlender, B. and Tetzeli, R. (2015). Becoming Steve Jobs. New York: Crown Business, p. 404.
2. Larcker, D.F. and Miles, S.A. (2010). : 2010 Survey on CEO Succession Planning. Stanford, CA. Retrieved from http://rockcenter.law.stanford.edu/wp-content/uploads/2010/06/CEO-Survey-Brochure-Final2.pdf.
3. Lashinsky, A. (2012). Inside Apple: How America's Most Admired—and Secretive—Company Really Works. New York: Business Plus, p. 156.
4. Isaacson, W. (2011). Steve Jobs. New York: Simon & Schuster, p. 557.
5. Isaacson, W. (2011). Steve Jobs. New York: Simon & Schuster, p. 558.
6. Isaacson, W. (2011). Steve Jobs. New York: Simon & Schuster, p. 360.
7. Lashinsky, A. (2012). Inside Apple: How America's Most Admired—and Secretive—Company Really Works. New York: Business Plus, pp. 92–93.
8. Lashinsky, A. (2012). Inside Apple: How America's Most Admired—and Secretive—Company Really Works. New York: Business Plus, p. 91, 95.

9. Lashinsky, A. (2012). Inside Apple: How America's Most Admired—and Secretive—Company Really Works. New York: Business Plus, p. 96.
10. Lashinsky, A. (2012). Inside Apple: How America's Most Admired—and Secretive—Company Really Works. New York: Business Plus, p. 95.
11. Isaacson, W. (2011). Steve Jobs. New York: Simon & Schuster, p. 361.
12. Isaacson, W. (2011). Steve Jobs. New York: Simon & Schuster, p. 458.
13. Lashinsky, A. (2012). Inside Apple: How America's Most Admired—and Secretive—Company Really Works. New York: Business Plus, p. 91.
14. Lashinsky, A. (2012). Inside Apple: How America's Most Admired—and Secretive—Company Really Works. New York: Business Plus, p. 89.
15. McGregor, J. (2016, August 13). Tim Cook, the interview: Running Apple 'is sort of a lonely job. *Washington Post.* Retrieved from http://www.washingtonpost.com/sf/business/2016/08/13/tim-cook-the-interview-running-apple-is-sort-of-a-lonely-job/.
16. Reisinger, D. (2016, August 24). These are the top highlights from Tim Cook's 5 years as Apple's CEO. *Fortune.* Retrieved from http://fortune.com/2016/08/24/tim-cook-apple-ceo-five-years/.
17. Booton, J. (2016, August 28). 5 things Tim Cook has done better at Apple than Steve Jobs did. *MarketWatch.* Retrieved from http://www.marketwatch.com/story/5-things-tim-cook-has-done-better-than-steve-jobs-2016-08-24.
18. Elmer-De Witt, P. (2017, August 4). Where Apple services would fit in the Fortune 100. *Apple 3.0.* Retrieved from https://www.Ped30.com/2017/08/04/apple-services-fortune-100/.
19. Biggs, J. (2017, September 13). It's not hard to beat Rolex, Apple. *Tech Crunch.* Retrieved from https://techcrunch.com/2017/09/13/its-not-hard-to-beat-rolex/.
20. Rose, C. (2015, December 20). What's next for Apple. *60 minutes.* Retrieved from http://www.cbsnews.com/news/60-minutes-apple-tim-cook-charlie-rose/.
21. Schlender, B. and Tetzeli, R. (2015). Becoming Steve Jobs. New York: Crown Business, p. 406.
22. Schlender, B. and Tetzeli, R. (2015). Becoming Steve Jobs. New York: Crown Business, p. 391.
23. Isaacson, W. (2011). Steve Jobs. New York: Simon & Schuster, p. 488.
24. Tetzeli, R. (2016, August 9). Tim Cook on Apples' values, mistakes and seeing around corners. *Fast Company.* Retrieved from https://www.fastcompany.com/3062595/tim-cooks-apple/tim-cook-on-why-apple-still-matters.
25. Rothwell, W.J. (2010). Effective Succession Planning: Ensuring Leadership Continuity and Building Talent from Within. New York: Amacom.
26. Blodget, H. (2011, October 25). Steve Jobs to Tim Cook: Don't do what I would do—Just do what's right. *Business Insider.* Retrieved from http://www.businessinsider.com/steve-jobs-to-tim-cook-dont-do-what-i-would-do-just-do-whats-right-2011-10.
27. Elmer-Dewitt, P. (2010, August 13). Why Steve Jobs Doesn't pay Dividends. *Fortune.* Retrieved from http://fortune.com/2010/08/13/why-steve-jobs-doesnt-pay-dividends/.
28. Baldwin, W. (2012, March 19). Steve Jobs wouldn't have paid a dividend. *Forbes.* Retrieved from http://www.forbes.com/sites/baldwin/2012/03/19/steve-jobs-wouldnt-have-paid-a-dividend-3/2/#7f20a13848cc.
29. Sarno, D. and Guynn, J. (2012, March 20). Apple's decision to pay dividends shows imprint of CEO Tim Cook. *Los Angeles Times.* Retrieved from http://articles.latimes.com/2012/mar/20/business/la-fi-apple-cook-20120320.

30. Digler, D.E. (2016, May 10). Apple Inc. shares reach ex-dividend as it gears up to distribute $2.9 billion to shareholders. *Appleinsider*. Retrieved from http://appleinsider.com/articles/16/05/10/apple-inc-shares-reach-ex-dividend-as-it-gears-up-to-distribute-29-billion-to-shareholders.
31. Apple. (n.d.). Environment. *Apple*. Retrieved from http://apple.com/enviroment.
32. Apple. (n.d.). Environment. *Apple*. Retrieved from http://apple.com/diversity.
33. Lashinsky, A. (2015, March 26). Apple's Tim Cook leads different. *Fortune*. Retrieved from http://fortune.com/2015/03/26/tim-cook/.
34. Sorkin, A.R. (2011, August 29). The Mystery of Steve Jobs' Public Giving. *New York Times*. Retrieved from http://dealbook.nytimes.com/2011/08/29/the-mystery-of-steve-jobss-public-giving/?_r=1.
35. Caufiled, B. (2011, September 8). Apple to match employees' charitable contributions. *Forbes*. Retrieved from http://www.forbes.com/sites/briancaulfield/2011/09/08/apple-to-match-employees-charitable-contributions/.
36. Charara, S. (2016, September 8). Tim Cook: Apple is the No. 2 watchmaker in the world (behind Rolex). *Wareable*. Retrieved from http://www.wareable.com/apple/watch-sales-rolex-tim-cook-556.
37. Northouse, P.G. (2013). Leadership. Thousand Oaks, CA: Sage, pp. 77–83.
38. Schlender, B. and Tetzeli, R. (2015). Becoming Steve Jobs. New York: Crown Business, pp. 392–393.
39. Tetzeli, R. (2016, August 8). Playing the Long Game Inside Tim Cook's Apple. *Fast Company*. Retrieved from https://www.fastcompany.com/3062090/tim-cooks-apple/playing-the-long-game-inside-tim-cooks-apple.
40. Yarow J. (2012, December 6). Tim Cook: Why I Fired Scott Forstall. *Business Insider*. Retrieved from http://www.businessinsider.com/tim-cook-why-i-fired-scott-forstall-2012-12.
41. Tetzeli, R. (2016, January 27). Apple's Angela Ahrendts on what it takes to make change inside a successful business. *Fast Company*. Retrieved from https://www.fastcompany.com/3055415/apples-angela-ahrendts-on-what-it-takes-to-make-change-inside-a-successful-business.

CHAPTER 11

1. Hsieh, T. (2010). Delivering happiness. Retrieved July 10, 2013, from http://www.slideshare.net/Vator/tony-hsieh-delivering-happiness.
2. Meyer, D. (2008). Setting the Table. New York: Harper, p. 2.
3. Schlender, B. and Tetzeli, R. (2015). Becoming Steve Jobs. New York: Crown Business, p. 413.
4. Schultz, H. and Yang, D.J. (1997). Pour Your Heart into It. New York: Hachette Books, p. 19.
5. Lashinsky, A. (2012). Inside Apple: How America's Most Admired—and Secretive—Company Really Works. New York: Business Plus, p. 60.
6. Kahney, L. (2008). Inside Steve's Brain. New York: Penguin Group, p. 41.
7. Kalpan, S. (2017). *The Invisible Advantage: How to Create a Culture of Innovation*. Austin, TX: Greenleaf Book Group Press, p. 9.

Index

W

Wayne, Ron, 42
Wozniak, Steve
　Apple II and its improvements, 42
　gifted at programming, 40
　hardware designer, 40
　improving Apple II, 43
　Jobs relationship, 40–41
　near fatal-accident of, 43
　techno-wunderkind, 40

Z

Zappos
　customer care, 64
　delivering happiness, 66–67
　going tribal, 65–66
　hiring, 65
　Hsieh's attention, 63–64
　market leader, 63–64
　Venture Frog, 63